"Asara Lovejoy brought her innovative, Commanding Wealth® program to our team with hugely motivational and beneficial results. Our Consultants had a record year and increased their income two to three times. We won more business than we pitched for by putting what Asara taught us into practice."

-Moira Benigson, President - Executive Search, UK

"Working with Asara from the inception of our business in imagining what was possible, clearing our limiting beliefs, and refocusing our energy into making it happen, has brought us a multimillion-dollar business that we started from just an idea. We celebrate!"

-Anna Pauly, President - Kriana Corporation

"At first it was hard to believe that The One Command® was actually increasing my income and my business. After a continuous increase in cash - paying off $45,000 in debt and making more than $90,000 in income, I now believe! And it can work for you too."

-Aeron Goldheart, CEO - America Choose Love

The One Command

The One Command

© 2007 Asara Lovejoy
Author Photo by Jason King
Cover by Aileen Yost
Interior by Chad Snyder

HB ISBN 13: 978-0-9791263-3-8
HB ISBN 10: 0-9791263-3-9
PB ISBN 13: 978-0-9791263-4-5
PB ISBN 10: 0-9791263-4-7

LCCN 2007939797
First Edition
1 2 3 4 5 6 7 8 9 10

For information, please contact:

Wisdom House Books
the vehicle for your vision

15455 Dallas Parkway, Suite 600
Dallas, Texas 75001
Tel. 214-566-9590 or Toll Free 866-583-9969
www.wisdomhousebooks.com

A POWER WITHIN YOU SO GREAT...

The One Command

COMMAND YOUR WEALTH...

IMPRINT YOUR DNA FOR
LASTING SUCCESS AS YOU
DISCOVER RICH PORTIONS OF
YOUR MIND THAT CREATE
WEALTH AND SATISFACTION!

Asara Lovejoy

This book is dedicated to my children,

Eden, Lee, Richard, and Ananda,

who have the depth and breadth of character, and graciousness of spirit to forgive me my mistakes.

Table of Contents

SECTION I: Foundation   1

SECTION VII: Unwinding   139

Acknowledgments

I wish to thank the many who have shared their wisdom and help on the journey:

Kathryn Perry, who has traveled every step, side by side; Joanna Gest, who has always believed; Michael Gest, for his wisdom and spiritual guidance, much of which is between these pages; Dr. Gowri Motha, for demonstrating the real healer; Paul Rebillot, Ze Miranda, Shirley Barclay, and Vianna Stibal for amazing teachings; Jerry Richardson, for new ways of thinking and learning to talk softly; Sandy Breckinridge and Kirk VandenBerghe, for training the brain and the heart; Richard Cuadra, Stephany Murdock, and Greg Simmons, for the beginnings; Bonnie Strehlow, for the many hours of changing beliefs: and Jason King, for the continuous creative Web design and back-end support.

I especially wish to say thank you with great gratitude to the many wonderful friends who made it all possible along the way: Donna Aazura, Peter Adamson, Hannelori and Curt Allina, Victoria and Marty Askin, Donna Baverman, Maureen Bell, Bonnie Bergan, Moira and Victor Benigson, Michele Blood, Benedickte and Miguel Cuadra, Steve Fedorka, Seb Francis, Toni Franks, Aeron Goldheart, Dr. Yehudi Gordon, Tracy Holloway, Ulrika Jensen, Jenny Johnston, Dot Kaufman, Bob Keeton, Diane Laird, Lila Lear, Hilde McCarthy, Rob Mottram, Alex Newman, Kris and Anna Pauly, Eve Powell and Orio, John Pultro, Mark Rainey, Vicky and Dan Renia, Nancy Seals, Kynette Shields, Cynthia and David Rigby, Terri Jo Summer, Reit Warmerdam, Joyce West,

Victoria West, Gayle Zane-Wilson, Woody Woodward, Alex Wren, and Emily Zephernick.

A special thank you to Aileen Yost for the beautiful book cover and especially Annette Maxberry-Carrara, Christine Frank, Chad Snyder, and Deanne Lachner at Wisdom House Books. Posthumously, with great love and admiration, thank you Jack Schwarz for setting the standard for the path, and Keith Hanson, for NLP and transformation.

About This Book

The simple premise of this book is that you have the capacity within you to change your life. That capacity is found within unused portions of your brain that you activate through a simple Six-Step Process that teaches you to lower your brain waves to theta. This ability has always existed, but until recently, only those few who have dedicated years of their lives to the process have been able to go consciously into the theta state while awake. Theta is naturally found to be most active while we are asleep. The benefits of consciously going in and out of theta are numerous.

In theta, you reconnect to your natural, creative intelligence, and disengage from the fearful, limited world view of what is possible. You develop a natural sense of security and trust in the world. The thoughts you have while in theta are more powerful than your ordinary thoughts, and they bring about changes in your life quickly and easily.

This book shows you that living life while using another portion of your brain is possible, and highly desirable. At another level, it explains how we think and act in our "humanness," enabling us to better understand the journey we are taking together, and to discover new ways in which we can grow and change.

Most of the material in the book was brought to me while in the altered state of theta. As a result, there is often a repetition of the words, with a beat and cadence that is purposeful, to activate knowledge from within you.

You may read this book in many ways. You may simply read it as a good story and still receive much knowledge at a deep, unconscious level within you. You may read for a while and then pause before starting again. There are layers of information that make changes in your brain and body that often take time to integrate and digest. Or you may read the book again and again and realize a great transformation in your ability to be rich and prosperous and happy and satisfied.

It is almost mysterious to me how I can open the pages and every time another new concept and a greater understanding are shown to me. In many ways, this book has a very real life of its own.

This book has been written to make a difference in our lives. With the greatest and highest regard, I respect your knowledge of how you best enjoy its purpose.

Words from the Author

How many times have you heard that your negative thoughts are the cause of financial lack and limitation? Or, if you are rich, the fear of losing what you have has kept you from a peaceful enjoyment of your wealth? And why is it that with every effort to change these conditions it hasn't quite worked yet?

The answer, I discovered, is because the most powerful yet mostly ignored portions of our mind—the ones that can change our limited ideas into a rich life lived with grace and ease—have been left untapped.

The realization of this great capacity and the ability to create a rich life while engaged there changed my income and fortune from fear of lack and financial stress to a life of prosperity and happiness. When I discovered that greater capacity, it guided me in my every effort to be rich, joyful, and prosperous and removed forever that never-ending financial struggle that many of us have experienced.

I discovered that there are many levels to what we think is true about cash, money, and financial independence. Most of our ideas are based on the thought that there won't be enough, or that money seems elusive and difficult to obtain, or, if we are rich, that we will lose what we have, or others may take it from us.

Many can argue that reality is as it is, but it is my experience that the opposite is exactly true: reality is ours for the making.

While reading this book, you will discover something powerful and new. This book does have the answer to stopping your negative, limiting thoughts and creating successful, prosperous ones instead. It is a simple process known as The One Command.

You can use this one simple process to bring increased good into your life in the form of more cash, payment of your debts, better relationships, or a greater sense of peace of mind.

The One Command has three parts. The first part stops your old way of negative or fearful thinking; the second part puts your mind into a state of p a u s e where you connect to that greater capacity within you; and the third part brings your dreams and desires to the world.

As you master this simple procedure, you add other ingredients, such as the powerful technique of reversing debt into the flow of a rich life coming to you. You discover there is a new way to learn and to establish new relationships with cash and wealth.

You discover the easy way to accept knowledge directly into your body, your emotions, your mind, and your DNA itself. I know that it may sound far fetched to think that you can learn something in a new way without struggle and strife, but you can. It is provable, with demonstrable results from those who are using these techniques.

One woman who attended our public seminar, Commanding Wealth®, left Sunday afternoon for a simple preliminary business discussion and unexpectedly received a $30,000 contract right on the spot. Folks reading this material are receiving cash and checks in the mail. Time speeds up in producing the beneficial results you intend—in some cases, almost instantly.

This teaching works because the way of thinking and creating I discovered is in actuality the most natural way of thinking and being that there is. It is, in fact, more natural to succeed, to be peaceful, and to live without stress. You learn here that the simple reason you may not be living this kind of life yet is that you have been trained not to. When you undo your negative, fearful training, you can come back into a more natural way of thinking and being: the way of the rich and contented.

What you discover here can change your life, allowing you to live richly and to prosper easily. It can change the cells of your body and your DNA to know what it feels like to be peaceful and prosperous; to be a good, kind, generous person who is rich; to be spiritual and rich; to do more with your life; and to experience greater satisfaction as you help others.

In these pages, you learn that these ideas are more than possible and that in fact they are the truth of who you are.

Many programs tell you what is needed to change your financial future, but this material teaches you to reorganize your emotions, your thinking, and the cells of your body to achieve your success.

If you are willing to set aside your notions of what you think you know, and if you are open to taking an incredible new adventure, then The One Command will forever alter your concepts of money and will increase your financial good.

This information goes beyond anything that you have known before. It makes changes in your physical brain by creating new neuro-net pathways for prosperity and joy, at the same time it closes your current poor, stressful receptor sites to lack forever.

The advanced process of connecting to that greater capacity within you, which I call your Source Mind, and receiving new emotional understanding by directly linking to your prosperity and good, is the power that actualizes every cell of your body and your DNA to a new, money-rich chemistry.

If you believe that you know how the world of money and finance operates—that you have to work hard, struggle, save, and invest wisely to create your financial security—then this information will change your mind forever. While it is good to invest wisely, you learn there is a greater secret to your true wealth. Those who have embraced these principles have all experienced the same beneficial results: an increase in prosperity, security, and joyful living.

It can be fun to create cash and to change your emotional poor-thinking to rich-thinking and to change your fearful money thoughts to financially secure and peaceful thoughts.

You discover that as you release your money fears, you have space to reprogram your inner thoughts and feelings and your DNA to accept prosperity, naturally and easily.

Do not read this information for advice.
The information here is knowledge that, as you embrace it, will change your every concept of how to live richly.

If you want to operate your own power equipment, and become the engineer of your future, then this material is for you.

If you are rich, yet want something more in terms of peace of mind, satisfaction, and removal of fear from losing what you have, then this information is for you.

If you have enough, and want more, then this is for you.

If you have never had enough, and are constantly on the brink of financial difficulty, then this is for you.

Throughout this book, you will enjoy the sound of prosperity in every cell of your body, intellect, and spirit, as you bring that level of wealth that you desire to you as yours to keep and to enjoy.

Whether you are rich, struggling financially, or in between, you will find new, amazing ideas and techniques that establish great money chemistry, as well as joy, pleasure, and stability in your financial life. Welcome to a new way of achieving your dreams.

Introduction

The knowledge in The One Command arrived in my life at a pivotal point. My mom had passed on, and I received an inheritance. Along with the money I had saved, I had a considerable amount.

My dream was to move to beautiful Whidbey Island, Washington, to create a healing retreat for the benefit of myself and others. I found and purchased the perfect property, which I knew had the potential to shine with "a little fixing up." I was eager to implement my dreams.

I jumped into the project with love and expectations of turning the home and the grounds into the beautiful center I imagined. I operated with considerable optimism, but little practical knowledge, and for two years, I remodeled and built.

Once started, the demands of the remodel took on a life of their own until, not only had I spent every penny that I had, but I had to borrow on the house and put myself into debt to finish what was started just to make the home livable. As a result, I had no cash, huge debt, and a large monthly mortgage. I also had no income because I had quit working during the two years it took to remodel the home.

I woke up one morning, after a stressful night of no sleep, with a horrible feeling of doom and desolation, and as my body shook in fear and distress, I collapsed onto the ground in true anguish over my circumstances.

"I do not want to be here again," I moaned. My pattern of having lots of money and then going broke was repeating itself once again.

"I am ruined," I thought, "and probably will be homeless and have to work hard for the rest of my life just to keep a small apartment. What a disappointment I am to myself, and what a financial mess I have made of my life."

As I lay crumpled on the floor, I had the thought that because I had been so blessed with a rich ex-husband who gave me child support for years, and a family that bailed me out financially on many occasions, I had never truly understood the principle of creating money from my own ingenuity and that greater capacity we all have within us. I thought that getting financial "bail-out" money was the answer.

I was so devastated that I had "blown" my last chance for a good life—that I had spent every dime of my fortune, had no income, no career to produce any income, and a large mortgage, that I didn't want to continue living. "I can't and won't live in poverty and struggle for the remainder of my life, just to make ends meet," I thought to myself. I wanted to die. I told myself I'd rather leave the planet than live that kind of life. "And in addition," I told myself, "I am too old to change anything anyway."

With those thoughts, I heard what I was really saying: that I wanted my old way of being to die; I wanted the struggle of earning money and keeping money to die.

I knew that my old way of thinking and prospering had brought me to this moment. If I looked at the facts of my circumstances, then I knew that I would be defeated—there was no quick fix or rational thought with which I could imagine a solution. I had no job, I had no income, I had no money or surplus of money, had borrowed the maximum I could, and I had looming expenses and debts.

This was the moment I changed my old way of thinking and the subconscious programs that had kept me from my financial good.

Up until this moment, as I worked over the years, whatever

considerable amount of cash and income I had produced was never enough. Any time I got ahead, I created some experience that left me behind financially. In the past, I had gone to my family to borrow money; now that wasn't available, so what could I do? I truly did not know how, nor could I figure out the answers with my small human brain.

In this moment of hopelessness, I surrendered my old ideas of how to create my financial good and embraced the radical concepts that you will hear about in this teaching, the very techniques that can and will change your financial destiny for the better forever. I came to know, as you can come to know, that outside circumstances do not create our destiny. Rather, the inside forces of our creative intelligence, and our ability to think, dream, and manifest from that greater capacity within us, which I call our Source Mind, are the providers of all our good. You can come to know financial good and prosperity, in greater measure than you can imagine at this moment, as yours. And if you are rich right now, you can come to know the joy of your riches, lived daily, with grace and ease.

By surrendering my old way of thinking, I came to know the simple One Command and Six-Step Process that created my wealth the easy way. One that has brought me greater financial good in my life than I have ever known. By the simple process of lowering my brain wave to the theta brain frequency, and creating from my Source Mind the unlimited potential of all that is, I manifested cash, income, relationships, health, and all that I could ever want or need in great abundance. In addition, I came to know the ancestral causes of lack, poverty, and our inability to enjoy a rich state of wealth, once wealth is ours.

My first test was to keep my home, the one in which I had invested all my financial resources and a great deal of love. Because I didn't have any logical answers on how to keep my home, or how to bring in enough money to pay my large mortgage within two weeks, there was no option other than to surrender and to trust the new method I was embracing to solve my financial problems.

I immediately practiced The One Command and the Six Steps to connect to that greater capacity within me, to my Source Mind, and I realized that I was actually changing my brain from the fast, ordinary thoughts that we call our beta waking consciousness, to the deeper, quieter brain frequency of theta. The quieting of my mind was the key to reversing my lack, fear, and limitation.

Over the next few days, as I engaged in practicing The One Command, the idea to lease my home to cover the mortgage came to me. By leasing, I could keep my home, even though I wouldn't be living there for a while, and I could give myself time to rebuild my income. Once I engaged in that idea, I took action and approached some local realtors for help. Their response was very negative: they said that what I wanted was impossible. The highest amount they had ever leased a home for on beautiful Whidbey Island was for $1600, they told me. They said that was tops. But this was a couple of thousand dollars short of my needs.

Rather than becoming discouraged, I immediately repudiated their notion of reality and instead stated The One Command: I don't know how I lease my home for three thousand dollars or more a month. I only know that I do now, and I am fulfilled.

I felt a great calm and peacefulness come over me when I reached that moment. I knew I had no control over anything; realtors didn't even give me hope, and the only thing I had left was faith that in spite of all outside circumstances, I could have what I declared and Commanded to be true. I had to act from the faith of creating a solution from that greater capacity within me. There was no other solution.

Once that moment arrived, I continued to state The One Command and wait for inspiration. I was guided to go on the

Internet and advertise my home for lease. Rather quickly, I received responses from individuals who thought the amount I requested was bargain rent for what the home had to offer. By the time my mortgage was due, I had a signed lease with the right tenant, which made it possible for me to keep my home, as well as a security deposit that gave me operating money to stay on my feet while I began to rebuild my career.

Today I am once again living in my beautiful home, and succeeding in every aspect of my life as I apply The One Command to create and manifest my financial success and emotional well-being. I invite you to open your mind to these new ideas of what is possible in your life. If I can do it by using this information to change my financial destiny, then so can you.

SECTION I
Foundation

Have I dreamed of late; of the person I want to be.
Have I renewed of late; my vision of the world I want to live in;
my dreams shall not crash down. My visions go not glimmering.
So long as I have breath, I know I have the strength to transform
what I can be to what I am.

- Unknown

Chapter One

Live in the Extraordinary

I have been a student of life, I have been a student of science and metaphysics, I have been a student of consciousness, I have been a teacher of mind-body courses, I have been an entrepreneur in many ventures, and I have owned my own university of learning.

When I reached the point-moment of surrendering to everything I had previously known about my prosperity, and there was no other choice in my life except to let go of my old ways of thinking or perish, I asked: "What is required for me to live differently? What is required for me to achieve what I desire?" All the information in the world hadn't gotten me there yet.

The doorway to a new understanding opened when I came to that dark night of the soul and sincerely sought an answer—when I let go of my old way of thinking, surrendered to a greater capacity within me, and discovered an extraordinary skill in my ability to create and manifest all the financial and emotional richness that I desired.

On many levels, it was a forced choice. It was either go forward in a new way, or return to the cycle of attempt, achieve, and defeat. How many of you have had that experience of those financial cycles: attempt, achieve, defeat? Or attempt, succeed, and then fear having it taken from you? These seem to be cycles we often repeat.

When we get stuck in our thinking, it is because we have been trained to think in a limited way, and yet I imagine that each and every one of you, just like me, has big dreams and desires that you wish to fulfill.

At the moment I surrendered, I discovered there was a way out of my old, limiting ideas. The way out was to engage in that portion of my brain that had not been programmed with any notions or ideas of what was possible: that greater capacity we all have within us, our Source Mind.

The knowledge I share with you right now can help you realize your dreams. This knowledge explains how we think, reason, and feel from a new perspective and tells us that we have control over our thoughts, now as never before. We have control now as never before because we have raised our levels of awareness and knowledge to include the abstract ideas of reality rather than just fixed notions.

In the abstract ideas of reality, the use of our imagination that energizes our thoughts is given as much prestige as linear, rote learning. In addition, from a quantum-thinking viewpoint, the position of our self as the observer or the "witness" of our own life is recognized as an effective tool in making new choices and implementing change.

One woman who embraced these teachings said, "As a child, I always criticized my sister because she was the dreamer who imagined many possible futures. I told her to get real and to learn to live in the 'real' world. Now it turns out that she knew more than I did. With these teachings, I go to my Source Mind through my imagination, and with The One Command, I manifest all my dreams, and then I implement my dreams through my logical skills. This is a blessing of all of who I am."

Discover Something New

I am excited that, by investigating this information, you are giving yourself a chance to discover something new about yourself, to discover your capacity to open your mind, and to activate new portions of your brain to manifest what you desire and to live in an extraordinary manner.

By connecting to that greater capacity within you, you can come to realize everything you truly are, to manifest your dreams, and love yourself in new ways.

You have a chance to discover who you are as wealthy and rich, rather than limited and fearful. You are enlightened, in that you are attracted to changing your life in this way, and you desire to make yourself fulfilled right now, in this physical body, in this experience of yourself. You desire to manifest from the unmanifest world, and to know the power within you to manifest from the unmanifest world, on a conscious basis, daily in your life, and to come forward and create more and more of what you desire, whether it is greater cash and riches, greater emotional satisfaction, or a betterment of relationships with your friends, family, and children.

Whatever it is that you are wishing to manifest, you learn to manifest with the simple yet powerful process of The One Command. You discover how to connect to that part of your brain that is there waiting to be activated, to be turned on, to be lit up, to be enlightened:to be able to say I have this capacity, and I am going to use it now; it is achieved.

Remember What You Know

There is much here that will effect great changes in you as you release old ideas and beliefs about who you are, and about the fabric of reality itself. As you awaken to the truth of who you are, you can become that which you have always known you were, that person who would someday arrive. That time is now.

As you remember what you know, you experience that remembrance. It is now possible to lift the veiled threat of a world reality based on fear and doubt, and to come home to what you have always known, the higher truth of your being. You can respond to the knowledge of your inner world, rather than to the chaos and limitations of the outer world.

The wake-up call is here for you to know that feelings of separation and fear are manmade, and that you are more than manmade; you are immortal beings of consciousness, and creators of your own life and destiny. The wake-up call is for you to become all that you are. A young man from Alaska who was graduating from a trade school in Montana said it well: "I have to go back home because there are too many fences here. Too many fences in people's thinking and not enough open space." Too many fences in the states of mind, the dogma fences, the political ideology fences, corporate fences, feuding fences, fear and limitation fences—too many fences.

We are remembering something bigger and grander than the fences. We are remembering the open space of our potential to create any reality we choose. We can reclaim those parts of us that have lost the ability to go up to another human being; to go up to ourselves; to go up to that part of us that is alive and trusting; to go up to that greater capacity within us, our Source Mind, the part of us that knows the truth of who we are; and to become the person who creates wealth and riches simply from knowing that we can.

This knowledge is about remembering who you are, even to the level of your DNA and the cells of your body, to live a rich, prosperous life, and to fulfill your rich dreams now. This knowledge is a practice, which, once embraced, can be used every day of your life to change your life for the better. The techniques in this practice are to remind you every day where you are going and what you are becoming—the masters of your life in a new way.

When you are in this state of remembrance, your world works. Your world works to your best advantage and to the best advantage of those in your world. These practices bring even more than you can imagine: instant money, open doors. You are heard, seen, responded to, embraced, well-paid, richer, loved, and joyful—every day. Struggle, effort, chaos, limitation, poorness, anger, and resentment (mine and yours) become ideas in the past, while what you desire to manifest becomes the next natural event in your life.

How often have you heard that we use only fifteen percent of our brain? Have you ever thought, "What about that other eighty-five percent of my brain that I am not using?" This is what it is for: that other eighty-five percent is to master your life, your way, now!

A Great Ability

When you learn to travel to your Source Mind through the Six-Step Process and when you issue The One Command, you activate portions of your brain that have been waiting to wake up. In doing so, you tap into ideas that are greater than you.

When you have an idea that is greater than you, you are increasing your capacity to think, to reason, to imagine the unknowable, and to manifest efficiently all that you desire.

When you live from this greater capacity within you, your limiting ideas of the world are diminished and naturally have less power over your thoughts and emotions. By placing your attention on what you wish to create, and by doing so in the powerful state of theta, it must become manifest.

It is not a question of whether you can manifest, because you already are. Yet what you are manifesting now is by and large not prosperity, greatness, and peaceful living. It is the opposite.

When you learn to think from that greater capacity within you ,and to allow ideas greater than you to arrive, you become the conscious director of your reality, and by doing so, you create your life anew.

Success Story

One woman I met came to me because she was in so much physical pain that she couldn't leave her home. Her back had been damaged years earlier, and the injury had caused acute and constant inflammation. At the same time, she was having this physical pain, her ex-husband was withdrawing his financial support—support that had maintained her comfortable lifestyle for years. She was terrified of the future. How would she survive?

She and I began by clearing many of her fearful beliefs by going through the steps to the theta state and declaring The One Command: I don't know how I am financially independent and maintain my lifestyle. I only know that I do now, and I am fulfilled.

Every time a negative and fearful thought would arrive, she would go into theta and restate The One Command: I don't know how I am financially independent and maintain my lifestyle. I only know that I do now, and I am fulfilled.

She began to have a sense of peace, even in her seemingly insurmountable difficulties, and soon her back pain disappeared. During this transition time, we held a Commanding Wealth® course that she also attended. She deeply engaged in shifting her fear of financial doom. The second day of the course, she came in, smiling and exclaimed, "I can't believe this, it is a miracle. I received a phone call from my ex-husband last night saying he had rethought our agreement and is going to give me six more months to get on my feet before stopping financial support, and there was an unexpected $3,000 check in the mail for me. What a blessing. I will now have time to restart my interior design career and to get on my feet."

Since those deciding moments of applying The One Command, she went from zero income to $350,000 for the year, and that indeed was a blessing. By her thinking in a greater capacity without evidence of the results, the results arrived as if by magic.

Chapter Two

An Idea Greater Than You

T here are many ways you can e x p a n d your thinking, and as a consequence improve your circumstances. The easiest method to increase your good in great measure is to let your mind imagine an idea even greater than you. To increase your wealth, prosperity and satisfaction, it is necessary to operate in another portion of your mind, one that knows a greater capacity than your everyday thoughts.

When you seek an idea that is greater than you while in the deep theta state and expand into something more, something unknown you create and manifest in the form and design of all the masters throughout the ages.

The power of this simple concept is a key to creating your financial riches and prosperity in an easy and effortless manner.

The rich abundance of cash, goods, emotional well-being, and financial success that you desire is all around you, in your atmosphere of creativity, of potential, and in the never-ending supply and substance of God matter.

Source is the substance of your good. Your thinking links you to the rich, abundant universe and makes manifest your rich, abundant life. As you are the power that is creating your reality right now, you have the power to manifest your financial good in new ways.

In the same way that you are unconsciously manifesting and

creating your limiting experiences, you can consciously create new experiences of money-rich prosperity, health, and happiness by expanding into an idea that provides greater good—good for others in addition to you, good beyond your ability to know it.

By being the willing participant of this greater good, you are blessed beyond measure. You magnetize and expand in such a large sphere of influence that you create a vacuum of power and magnetic attraction to you, and you pull that wonder of cash and riches right into your life and into your bank account.

Once you make room in your brain, in your mind, and in your thinking, then you receive more original thoughts, inspiring ideas, and creative ways to manifest cash and prosperity; at the same time, you experience that greater capacity of your mind and soul to create and magnetize to you all that you desire.

As you learn to consciously go into theta and your Source Mind, where the answer and solution to every situation exists, where new thoughts, ideas, inventions, and concepts are ready for you, then you become the master that you wish to be.

When you slow your mind to the theta brain frequency,
and consciously create from Source, you discover
how to reach the potential of everything that is possible.

Chapter Three

A Greater Sphere of Influence

I f you were to write down all of your thoughts, you would quickly see that you normally think in a very small circle of reccurring ideas, and as a result, you affect only a small sphere of influence. What you are learning here is to increase your sphere of influence by increasing your capacity of experience in the universe.

As you increase your model of reality, you allow a greater capacity of your good: those thoughts, feelings, and ideas of cash, prosperity, and emotional sanctity you desire to arrive. To allow your Source Mind to bring these experiences to you, you must rearrange your thoughts, even down to the microscopic level of your DNA, to let that happen. When you issue The One Command and receive new knowledge while connected to your theta mind, you accomplish a rearrangement of your thoughts, the cells of your body, and your DNA.

The One Command is a simple statement that stops your limited thinking, and creates a neutral space to redirect fear-based thoughts of lack with ones of abundance and constant supply, and then announces your intention to the universe.

The secret of masters throughout the ages is that by surrendering their own small thinking in their beta mind to a greater capacity, their Source Mind, they increase their sphere of influence and their riches in great measure.

You have the same ability to change your thinking to create a greater experience of prosperity, beauty, and harmony, and to increase your circle of influence. Each one of you is here to serve in some capacity.

Here, you are learning to align your heart to a greater measure and a greater sphere of influence. Once you discover this ability, everything in your life changes.

Your ability to manifest money in a greater capacity is the same ability for manifesting anything and everything that you desire: good health, relationships, success, happiness, and peace of mind.

Every moment is a choice of your reaction to your experience. When you react in old ways and familiar patterns of thought, you are thinking in a very small circle of influence. If you put your thoughts on paper, you would soon see a recurring theme and pattern of those thoughts—ones that circle and circle without increasing your capacity for new thoughts or ideas.

These recycling thoughts of limitation, and ideas such as, I have to struggle to be a financial success, or There isn't enough for me, are the beliefs that cause feelings of separation and pain. They are the very ones that can change now with the techniques you are learning.

When you change your small circle of unconscious thoughts to include new possibilities, you increase, abundantly, new thoughts and ideas of you and your prosperous life.

Success Story

A retired businessman was having financial difficulties and, because of his age, thought that he was stuck living poorly with very little. He had many negative thoughts about his circumstances and was unhappy in his thinking.

Through some friends, he discovered The One Command, and with their help, he gradually accepted the idea that it might work. As he said, "Nothing else has." He began to practice going into theta, Commanding his good, expanding the idea, and receiving his new experience directly into the cells of his body and his DNA.

He started with The One Command: I don't know how I receive additional income; I only know that I do now, and I am fulfilled.

A few days after he began to Command his financial increase, he received a knock on his door and opened it to find an old friend who had come by for a visit. After talking for a while, the friend said, without any prompting, "You know Steve I have been thinking about you lately, and I know I borrowed money from you when I wanted to start up my business and have never repaid you. I received a settlement recently and I have a check that I am happy to give you to repay the loan you gave me without hesitation." He handed the envelope to Steve.

That this money had seemingly come out of nowhere was so shocking to him that he continued with new Commands to improve his life, and shortly thereafter, he took a part-time job as an auto mechanic, something that he had always loved to do.

He increased his income; developed a better social life, and had more fun doing what he liked. Then he noticed one day that he often thought happy and peaceful thoughts, rather than negative and bitter ones, and he realized that he was living with a sense of fulfillment.

Chapter Four

Source Mind

O n my journey of "dying to my old way of thinking," I was continually directed to understand my ability to manifest and create within the subtle energy and expansive unlimited world of theta consciousness. I was shown that our Source Mind is greater than the human brain, and is the place from which we are creating and manifesting our desires.

The path to our Source Mind is by lowering our brain to the theta state. This state is the place our ideas and thoughts originate before they become conscious thoughts in our human minds. This process is a natural, unconscious process. What we are learning here is to consciously travel to our Source Mind to manifest what we desire.

By learning to go to that greater capacity within you, you can bring forth new ideas, and while in this higher state of consciousness, successfully Command your wealth and prosperity.

Source Mind is that part of your consciousness that is greater than your human brain, and the place from which you are, in actuality, creating your reality before it is known in physical form. It is from the unseen and the unknown that you are creating your life—before it becomes the seen and the known.

It is the place where your desires exist as pure energy, in their highest expression, before you have a conscious awareness in your human brain and before you bring that awareness into the physical world as matter.

When you think about the good you want to bring into your life in the highest form, you must travel to your higher Source Mind—the place wherein all ideas and new discoveries, throughout all the ages, originate and exist as potential.

It is that level of your thinking that cannot be known with your limited human brain, and can only be known by the evidence of what you manifest.

Engage Your Source Mind

The path to your prosperity and to changing your experience with cash, money, security, peace of mind, and joy is by engaging your Source Mind and disengaging from your human, fear-based, conditioned mind.

When you travel to Source, you learn to trust that what you know from this state is more real than what you have been taught in the mundane world.

When you create from the higher spiritual laws, you can instantly multiply supply, reverse debt, and neutralize the collective, agreed-upon, group-conscious mind of limited ideas and thoughts.

It is when you apply your spiritual mind to your prosperity thinking that you create miracles and attract cash into your life.

Prosperous Living

Prosperity brings an inner peace, self-confidence, a sense of self-worth, poise, happiness, security, and stability.

You are in contact with your Source Mind when you lower your brain frequency to the theta brain state.

It is natural for you to travel to theta and to create that which you desire. It is a matter of remembering what you have forgotten by your own free will and volition.

Source Mind is that place in your consciousness from which you are creating reality before it is known in physical form. It is from the unseen—the unknown—that you are creating before it becomes the seen and the known.

Your Source Mind often feels that you are more important than you do and is often more on your side than you are. Now you can reconnect to that powerful Source of your being, and by doing so, you can create all the good that you desire.

Many people who have reconnected to that loving and secure place report being in a state of comfort, quiet, and non-judgment, and they feel a greater sense of well-being each and every time.

One woman shares her experience on the Six-Step Process of connecting to Source.

"When I am in theta, in the presence of the Creator and this amazing place of unconditional love and all the potential of all that is, I find it hard to return to ordinary life. This is a place of peace I have always longed for. I find that when I do return, I have a sense of peace and security within me for longer and longer periods of time. Eventually, I have noticed that it has become my natural way of viewing the world. What a change."

We have come to that place in consciousness where we can now lower our brain wave to the theta state at will, and while there, we reach into our Source Mind and consciously create the life that we seek.

This process is a natural occurrence. It is natural to travel to your Source Mind and to create financial success and prosperity.

Instantly Create Your Good

When you consciously go into your Source Mind, you create instantly from your higher state and manifest quickly and easily.

By going to Source with the intention of having a prosperous experience, you shift your consciousness. Whatever you focus on in your consciousness must manifest. You are manifesting the thoughts that you are thinking now. That is why you are already masters: you are already manifesting what you are thinking. When you shift your thinking to rich and prosperous thoughts, you don't have to worry about whether they will manifest or not. They must. It is the law of attraction in action in a different direction, a rich and prosperous one.

Every religion or philosophy of spirituality has the common thread of this knowledge that you connect to a loving God and something greater than you for true happiness.

Here you are learning to empower yourself to make this journey to that state within you, as often and as frequently as you desire, and to train your brain in a new way. By going to your Source Mind, you learn to know who you are, and you live your life remembering who you are, and you have all the power and the creativity of your greater capacity to provide rich, sustaining rewards for your life.

If you are a spiritual person, this ability will seem familiar. If you do not consider yourself a spiritual person, then you will be entering into a new experience of a greater capacity within you to love, to trust, and to know the world as safe.

Success Story

A teenage girl and her mother were shopping at the mall together, and the daughter told her mom she wanted a job so she could buy herself some clothes. The mom had discovered The One Command and spontaneously said to her daughter, "Hey, I have been using this technique to manifest some things for myself, and I can show it to you if you want."

The daughter said "Okay" and her mom walked her through the Six Steps. She Commanded, I don't know how I have a job, I only know that I do now, and I am fulfilled.

While they were still talking about getting a job, they went into the daughter's favorite clothes store and the owner overheard their conversation. She spoke to the girl and said, "If you'd like a job here, fill out this application and I'll hire you. We are adding some staff this week."

The girl accepted the application and the job and left the store saying to her mom, "This is just too spooky Mom, but I like it."

Chapter Five

A Rich Change

When we talk about our Source Mind and going to theta, we are speaking about a particular brain wave and our consciousness as a state change—a state of consciousness as determined by what brain wave we are operating in at the moment.

When you change from one state of thinking, one brain wave to another, it is an internal, universal event everywhere within you, in a moment.

When you feel an emotion such as depression, excitement, fear or joy, everything in you is in a depressed state or an expressed state. Everything in you is in a fearful state or a joyful state. When you are thinking a thought of lack, or abundance and riches, everything in you is in a limited state or, in a prosperous state, or, a wealthy state. A state change means a change of consciousness.

When you have a thought in your brain, in a certain state of consciousness, your brain wave is emanating from you in all directions in a certain frequency, in a specific range.

Our brain waves are measured as micro-electrical charges in cycles per second. The ones we are most familiar with are: beta, 13–30 cycles per second, known as our waking conscious mind; alpha, measured at 7–13 cycles per second, known as our meditative and contemplative mind; theta, 4–7 cycles per second, our Source Mind; and delta, .01–4 cycles per second, the lowest brain frequency before death.

Your brain waves emanate from you in a radiance of subtle matter, much like invisible radio waves. You radiate out your thoughts and attract back to you your experience, only within that range of your consciousness. As you lower you brain waves to theta, you increase the range, amplitude, and altitude of your thoughts out into a greater and greater sphere of influence, in a grander and larger field of magnetic attraction, including more and more choices and possibilities.

For example, if you were to say that the beta brain wave, known as your ordinary thinking mind, has the capacity of solving problems and manifesting for you in all directions, then that range of thinking and problem solving could reach the equivalent of the country of England. You might think that is quite good, but in reality, that is the most limited and smallest sphere of influence you have, and it is tied to the fearful thoughts in the mundane world and the collective mind, at the same time you are looking for a solution. This is where you experience struggle and opposition, or stress over issues of yours and mine, or engage in any duality of stop and start, or yes and no.

We spend most of our thinking time, about 99%, attempting to "figure out" our problems in beta and create our good from that part of our consciousness with the least capacity to bring us solutions or to manifest cash and resources.

Our logical, thinking, beta mind is wonderful and useful for implementing the design of our desires and for creating the action steps necessary for their implementation, but it is the least resourceful state for attracting that next level of our achievement or unexpected gifts and miracles. By living in the beta mind, we limit ourselves to ordinary, mundane, fear-based thinking, rather than our extraordinary mastery.

Increased Capacity Equals Increased Good

With each lowered brain state, the next being alpha, you send out a request and receive knowledge and information for problem solving or manifesting your good in a greater sphere of influence. In the alpha state, you can say that you gather information equal to all the knowledge on the planet, out to the outer edges of our planet, where gravity meets the vacuum of space.

When you go into theta, you transmit and receive information from the equivalent of our universe, everything in our solar system and galaxy, and in delta, the lowest brain frequency before death, you change into such a state of subtle consciousness that we cannot even know the range of information we can receive.

Your Thoughts Are Your Reflection

Our experiences have been teaching us that our thoughts are real. Our thoughts are creating our reality. Our unconscious thoughts are creating our reality. When you desire to master your life and you haven't achieved that yet, there is a separation between your unconscious thoughts and the conscious thoughts of your desire. When you understand that every thought you think is operating within you at all times and is an expression of who you are in the world, attracting only information of like kind to you in its capacity or sphere of influence, then you understand how you are creating your reality.

Your thoughts are real and are reflected back to you as your experience, according to your capacity to regulate your brain. As you send out your thoughts from different levels of your awareness, from different brain frequencies and states of consciousness, you command the world to respond to you according to what you believe is possible. You are a master and this is the way that you create your life. Now you are discovering a way to bypass your ordinary limited view of life, beta thinking, and to reach into your extraordinary ability, theta thinking, for extraordinary results.

Connection to Source

While we are developing as an embryo, and as infants right at the moment of birth, our brain activity is in theta. We know Source as infants; we know that connection to Source in theta. We are born knowing unlimited love and infinite possibilities.

If you have ever been present at a birth, then you will have experienced that amazing love, that gentleness, and that feeling of light that you see around that infant. It is because you are experiencing the effects of the theta brain wave emanating from the infant to you. When a child is evolving in the consciousness of imagination, and he or she says "I see lights over there around that person," that child is seeing that greater capacity of who we are in the more subtle fields of energy to which they are still connected.

We are so much more than we can even comprehend. This teaching is returning us to that knowledge of our greatness, and even more than that. Do you want to play there? Do you want to create your life from there? I think so!

Chapter Six

Your Magnetic Thoughts

f you have meditated or practiced regular prayer, or any kind of contemplation, then you know that you have the capacity to quiet your ordinary, rapid beta mind to a lower cycle, such as theta. If you have never "formally" thought to quiet your mind, realize that when you daydream or are in deep thought, you are accomplishing the same thing.

We generate an electro-magnetic field of attraction or repulsion with our thoughts through the release, from our endocrine system, of hormones and chemicals known as peptides. We generate electro-magnetic charges with our thoughts that either attract to us or repel from us our experiences. Our thoughts travel through positive/negative receptors in every cell of our body and fire sequences in the neuro-net passages of our brain. These micro-electrical charges formed by our thinking are real. They influence our reality by magnetically attracting experiences of like kind to us in either a positive or negative manner, or by repelling experiences from us. Our unconscious thoughts that operate below our conscious awareness hold great power over our lives as they are firing the peptide messengers that unconsciously drive our choices.

When we desire to be masters and we haven't achieved it yet, there is a separation between the unconscious thoughts that are driving our choices, and the conscious thoughts of our desire.

When we understand that every thought we think operates within us, below our awareness every moment, expressing out into the world and attracting information of like kind through the energy of our electromagnetic thinking, then we understand how we are creating our lives.

Ordinary Thinking

It is important to note that we go in and out of many combinations of brain waves moment by moment, yet we can become more focused in one brain wave than another at will, even as we unconsciously operate in many frequencies daily.

The most frequently accessed brain wave, beta, that we use when we are talking and thinking, is where we also run endless programs of fear and doubt and limitation.

In the slower brain frequency of theta, we can control our thoughts, and access that great capacity of who we are. When we are in this state, we can manifest all of our good instantly. It is often unfamiliar when you connect to that wonderful part of you that is allowing, loving, supportive, and has only your best interests at heart, yet you can become easily addicted to accomplishing what you want and realizing your dreams by learning this state of you.

Your mind cannot hold two thoughts at the same time. As you begin to concentrate in another way on manifesting money, prosperity, compassion, and joy, your old way of thinking simply dissolves through lack of use. If you relax and train yourself to be open, with grace and ease, to another possibility of prosperity, then that is what you will create.

Extraordinary Thinking

As our wants and desires regulate our thinking through our feelings (micro-electrical charges), our emotional thinking can Command information from the Source of who we are in theta to manifest that in our human experience.

What you are learning now is conscious access to your theta state of extraordinary thinking. You are embarking on a journey to attain other levels of consciousness within you by consciously slowing your mind to theta. This process can become as easy and automatic as waking up in the morning and going to sleep at night.

The theta brain wave is the vessel of change from your ordinary, beta-thinking, worried state to your peaceful, theta, God Mind, and the path to your immeasurable good.

By going into theta consciously, you become the master of wealth you desire to become. It is that simple.

When we talk about the four brain waves—beta, alpha, theta, and delta—it is important to note that all brain waves are active in some capacity at all times. With very little practice in lowering your brain wave to the theta state and going to Source, you can investigate the many dimensions of who you are. Your greater capacity exists in such subtle energy of self that you can only know it in this relaxed theta state.

A great benefit of thinking in theta connected to Source is that you de-link from the limiting and fearful thoughts held in your subconscious mind and attract a greater, richly abundant truth without resistance, seemingly by magic.

Success Story

A wealthy businessman started to practice The One Command to reduce his anxiety and stress. His wealth had not brought him peace of mind or a sense of satisfaction. He had to be active all the time, going from one project to another to even like himself. Soon after he began lowering his brain to theta and issuing The One Command, he called me with good news.

"I am having the best sleep I have ever had in my life," he exclaimed, "and my family is much happier with me. We are going on a family vacation—an unusual event—and I am actually looking forward to taking the time off."

In addition, he reported that through the use of The One Command, a very difficult business transaction worth over $10 million dollars had closed. "I don't think anyone would believe me," he said, "if I told them I had Commanded this deal to come through."

Chapter Seven

You Create Your Life from Pure Energy

W ithin the Source Mind, there are higher spiritual, universal laws that are the basis of our lesser human ideas that embody the law of cause and effect, the chemistry of attraction and repulsion, and instant manifestation.

In science, these higher spiritual laws of creating something from nothing, or creating from the invisible substance of the universe to the visible, are known through the observation and scientific analysis of the universe's construction. Every day, new discoveries about the construction of the universe arrive. The substance of the universe, it is now known, is made of such small particles of matter that in actuality, substance is more like a thought than physical matter. This seemingly invisible something from which we create our life has the ability to know when it is observed, and to react to that observation.

What you have in your life now is a reflection of what you have brought into matter by your own thinking, with you in the role as the observer of your thoughts.

Because our thoughts are constructed of subtle energy, we are not aware that we are manifesting our lives from our Source Mind, yet we do so unconsciously moment by moment. When we think a thought and concentrate our attention, the law of consciousness sends that thought into our Source Mind, and from there, reflects it back to us in our daily experience. Because we are the observer of our own thoughts, only that which we think is possible may appear.

A Simple Story

One day there was a rag merchant whose donkey had died. He became very agitated because his ability to provide food for his family was gone if he couldn't drive his rag cart around the city to sell his rags. At the end of his street, there was a corral with an old, broken-down horse, and the rag merchant sent up a plea and a prayer to God and his angels to please, please let him have that broken-down old horse in order to survive.

Two of his guardian angels looked down at this good man and turning to each other, said, "He has specially asked for that old nag in the corral, so we have to give him what he requested, but I'd like to know what we are going to do with these two fine thoroughbred horses we had lined up for him instead."

If you find a limitation in your thinking that would bring you a broken down old nag rather than a pair of thoroughbreds, you may change it in a moment by going to your Source Mind and Commanding a new reality. It is that simple.

Chapter Eight

Your Wealth DNA

As you gain easy contact with your Source Mind, you activate your DNA for new programs of wealth. You shift, change, pull, and replace your limiting ideas with new concepts of health, happiness, richness, prosperity, and love; as you expand your circle of knowledge and influence, you truly live the life that you desire. It is the Law of Attraction in action. That is why your mastery of wealth is assured.

Your DNA and the cells of your body are genetically programmed for a greater understanding of life than you can imagine. Contained within your chromosomes are memories of all history, and all levels of life: mineral, plant, animal, atmospheric, other planets and worlds, biological, microbiological, human, spiritual, and the divine.

You are interacting daily in subtle ways with the memories and activity between these levels. You are much grander than you think you are. The trees in your area know who you are as you walk by, as do the plants, the minerals in the Earth, and the air you inhale and exhale.

You are known by your pets and other animals in your area, and you are connected with many thousands of individuals through out your life, and in your dream world.

Our small "pea brain," or human behavioral mind, is focused chiefly on the "this world" dimension.

Behind the scenes, you have an extraordinary capacity that is operating in many universes simultaneously. When you have an experience that gives you an understanding about life, you are relating that understanding to the universe on all levels.

In fact, the cells of your body organize themselves to comply in the future to bring about the reality that you are pulling towards you. This is how you create your future.

Your chromosomes and DNA attune themselves to your thoughts, beliefs, and desires, and then transfer that knowledge to all levels of life. Thus, you are impacting world reality with every choice you make. Your DNA also brings forward what it knows from the past, and integrates knowledge of that past with now.

Your DNA contains knowledge and wisdom that you have forgotten to remember, or have been trained to not allow in your memory and thoughts. Your DNA is a blessing of knowledge and wisdom, and it has helped you to design your life.

When you are structuring your life to become the master that you are, directly communicating with your DNA can instantly give you experiences that would normally take you lifetimes to understand.

The emotions and feelings of success and identity that you desire in your new world of plenty and riches can be yours instantly by directly linking to your DNA and activating the knowledge of these emotions.

What has been difficult in creating a new, rich, and prosperous identity for most people is the phenomenon of not knowing what that new experience would be like.

If you have always had a chaotic life, what would it feel like to live peacefully? Might you think that a joyful and rich life would be boring if you are used to upset and chaos? What if you could have a preview of what a rich, joyful, and interesting life would feel like?

By making a direct link with your DNA, you can activate the

knowledge and wisdom it contains.

When you are in theta, you can easily and readily communicate in all dimensions of who you are, even down to your DNA.

One woman applied The One Command: "I don't know how I increase my DNA for riches. I only know that I do now, and I am fulfilled." She went into the deep state of theta through the Six-Step Process and accepted this new understanding within the level of her DNA. As she came out of that deep state, her dog started barking and yipping at her as if he didn't recognize her. She laughed and told her dog, "Yes, it is still me. . .a new, rich me."

SECTION II
Six–Step Process

Chapter Nine

Source State Manifesting

Our body and mind cooperate to create our view of reality. It is now known that our DNA itself is altered by our thinking. The easy way to reprogram your emotional thinking about wealth, prosperity, and happiness is about to begin as you follow the simple Six-Step Process, connect to your Source Mind, and reconfigure your human-limited thinking to Source State Manifesting.

Connecting to your Source Mind is the key to retraining your thinking and feelings toward your financially rich life. It is the key because as you practice the Six Steps, you activate the knowledge in your body. Your body is the vessel of your emotions and thoughts, and it radiates your consciousness to the world. To change your feeling and thinking down to your DNA, you must teach your body what it feels like to have a new experience—a new experience of going to Source and creating everything you desire, consciously, in the field of pure energy.

As you send your thoughts and feelings out to magnetize your rewards back to you, you create a greater good than you can imagine. As you repeatedly practice this connection, you are literally developing new neuro-net pathways to bring that good to you consciously, quickly, and easily. You are opening your physical brain to your higher-dimensional Source Mind.

Some of you may have engaged in spiritual or meditative practices for years, and others may be experimenting with these states of awareness now for the first time. In either case, please know that it is necessary to physically practice the simple Six Steps to open new neuro-net pathways in your body and brain as you follow the model in this teaching.

It cannot be stated too strongly that you will have an amazing experience of understanding in a new way if you simply allow yourself to follow these easy and simple procedures. The activity in the physical body of stepping on each piece of paper in the Six-Step Process rewires your DNA and the cells of your body to know this information. It is training you at many levels of your being. Even if you are the most spiritual of masters, with years of meditation, this simple procedure is what is required to know this teaching. After your body has the opportunity to know the process of grounding, aligning, going to theta, Commanding, expanding, and receiving with gratitude, then you can activate the Six Steps internally, to manifest anything that you desire, instantly.

As you develop the skill to use your Source Mind, you operate more and more in the portion of your brain that is the key to your success in becoming a master of your thinking and your life. That is the portion of your brain that is not programmed with anything and is open to everything. The world view or your unconscious programs do not limit it. It is open to any possibility and new ideas that attract your greater wealth and good.

The more frequently you travel to your Source Mind by slowing to the theta brain frequency, the more and more of your brain you awaken, and the more mastery of wealth you achieve! By consciously going in and out of theta, you are able to connect to your Source Mind. As you do, notice your feelings, and the control and influence that you have in the process.

You are being directed to bring more and more harmony and order into your experience as you send your thoughts and feelings to that which you wish to create.

As you practice this connection, you are developing new neuro-pathways to bring that which you desire into manifestation—consciously, quickly, and easily—as you build a path in your physical brain.

As you travel to your higher-dimensional Source Mind, you may notice that your eyes roll up, even under your closed eyelids, and you may have some rapid eye movement as you slow your mind to your theta brain wave.

The part of your brain that you are activating regulates your eye muscles. It may seem as if you are straining your eyes as you activate this greater part of your brain, but any discomfort you may have is similar to what you would experience when exercising any new muscle. Masters have spent twenty to thirty years developing the skill you are now learning to do with very little effort. You have this capacity now because we have come to a new level of consciousness. You have the ability to embrace your greater self by simply doing it.

As with any new learning, be gentle on yourself. This process is real, and is teaching you to activate unused portions of your brain. The more frequently that you travel to your Source Mind by slowing your brain to theta, the more and more of your brain you awaken, and the more mastery you achieve.

Use Your Imagination

You are asked to use your imagination as you follow the steps to connect with Source. Everyone has a different style of imagining. There is no perfect or right way.

To begin, just accept that you are doing it, and eventually, you will know that you are connecting to Source and making great changes in your life.

If you need some evidence that you "can" imagine, close your eyes for a moment and think about an apple. See it as clearly as you can. Smell the scent and imagine the taste as you eat. Then open your eyes.

Now you know that you can use your imagination to follow the Six-Step Process.

The more that you go in and out of theta, the more capacity you have to create your life and to adjust your thinking. When you allow that greater capacity of who you are to guide your choices, you lift yourself above fear and old, subconscious programs, and you operate as a master.

If you were to know all that there is to know, then you could already understand that, in consciousness, you are creating the life you now have. You are not only creating the life you now have, you are manifesting daily the good and the difficult experiences that you have. When you seek a balance of understanding by reaching into a greater capacity of who you are, you operate from another dimension of self.

When thinking and feeling while in your Source Mind, you let go of your fearful thoughts, and you experience something different. . .something powerful, true, and real.

One woman reports her experiences in her own words, after applying The One Command:

"I have started a Wealth Journal, and what seems to be effortlessly pouring in are ideas, confidence, and knowledge in my own abilities. Just a few of the things I have manifested are an office to practice The Emotional Freedom Technique and Theta Healing, someone to present workshops with, easy journeys along busy roads and motorways, and extra money with relation to my job (small but very real amounts). My daughter has used The One Command to manifest a job and a strike at bowling (believe me, this last one astounded us all!!)."

Trust Knowing

The challenge has always been to trust that which you are knowing from you inner intelligence, rather than to trust what you know from what the world may tell you is real and true. You now have the ability to use portions of your brain that you may have never consciously accessed before.

In the past, there were a special few who, by the process of years of study and training, were able to go consciously into different brain waves, such as the theta brain frequency. Now you can do the same thing instantly, through the Six Steps.

A wealth master demonstrates manifesting that which she or he desires, such as cash, financial wealth, or any material good, by lowering her or his brain wave to theta and, while in this expanded state of consciousness, connecting directly with Source Mind and creating from the potential of All That Is.

Choose the Direction of Your Thoughts

Your thoughts are reflected around you in the circumstances of your life. Good, or not so good, that what you are creating in your life is done so by your thinking. Only you can change the direction of your thoughts to create something else, something more desirable. You can do this quite easily and most effortlessly when you are thinking about your desires in the theta brain state.

As you lower your brain wave to the theta frequency, you radiate a much more powerful signal that is received at a deeper level within those who are responding to you and your desires. The manifestation of your desires appears almost as if by magic—and quite quickly when you are in this state of thinking.

Those masters throughout the ages, able to accomplish miracles in healing and manifesting, were doing so from theta. The Six Steps are a simple process of going to theta, and, by issuing The One Command from this amazing place within you, you change your life to be rich and successful.

Success Story

One young woman had procured her "dream job" as a personal assistant to the president of a large business firm in Los Angeles. The woman was multi-talented in her ability to solve problems, keep communications current, respond quickly in emergencies, write and create forms, and formulate letters and back-end computer data to improve the president's response time to important clients and personnel. She did much more than what was required in her job description.

One day she was thinking about everything that she accomplished and had the idea that it would be great if she could receive a "bonus" for her skills in the same way those in upper management did. Now she realized that it was impractical to think about getting a "bonus" because that had never ever happened for someone in her job position.

However, she truly thought that it would be great if she received a bonus. She had been practicing The One Command and decided to Command a positive "bonus" for herself. She began with, "I don't' know how I receive a bonus for my work. I only know that I do now, and I am fulfilled."

She never mentioned the idea of a bonus to her boss or anyone at work. She simply Commanded that it be so.

Shortly thereafter, she was called into the president's office, and he complimented her on her great service and help in the many ways she had increased success for the company. He handed her an envelope he said, to show his appreciation.

Upon opening the envelope, she erupted in a scream of excitement. The envelope contained her personal "bonus" for $10,000.

Chapter Ten

The Six-Step Process

W hen you wish to create something for yourself, such as more income, a reduction of your debt, an increase of your available debt-free money, or a state of awareness such as more joy, peace of mind, better relationships or improved health, the first step in the process is to choose what you want to focus on to manifest or change.

Once you know what you wish to manifest, then you lower your brain to theta through the Six-Step Process, and while in a heightened state of conscious contact with Source, you state The One Command, and then return to ordinary consciousness, alert and refreshed in your physical body.

Engaging in the process actually heals cells of your body, revitalizes you, and increases your capacity to think and reason, in addition to training your brain to operate in this heightened, powerful state of awareness.

In this exercise, we ask you to "walk through" the procedure first so that your body learns it and knows it. There is a great power in physically digesting and teaching it to the cells of your body. Later, you will be able to simply go through the procedure mentally.

This is an experiential process, and it is best if you do this process with another person as a partner. When you are ready to begin, get six sheets of paper and write the following words on the sheets:

1. GROUND
2. ALIGN
3. GO TO THETA
4. COMMAND
5. EXPAND
6. RECEIVE WITH GRATITUDE

There is a knowing within your body that arrives as you step on each piece of paper for the six stages.

Lay out the six sheets of paper in a horizontal row. Close your eyes and keep them closed during the entire process. Your partner guides you to step sideways from one piece of paper to the next while he or she reads the instructions for each step. (What you actually read is found in the summation of the Six-Step Process in the Appendix.)

Take turns going through the process, first one partner then the other, and then repeat the procedure. Doing this process twice in your initial practice gives you a deeper understanding.

As one participant shares:

"Even though I am an energy worker and healer, and I do all kinds of phenomenal things with energy, I don't particularly feel them much in my body. Yet when it was time to go through the Six-Step Process and bring the energy through my body the first time, I really felt it come through. That was pretty exciting. I have to say it was more subtle but stronger the second time. What I was declaring the first time has been something I have had intentions on a number of times before. The first asking was kind of my minimum level, you know, and when we went to expand the idea to a greater capacity, it was the biggest level I have ever gone to. Previously, I have always had negative thoughts going off behind my requests and desires. This time, none of that negativity was real. I take and accept my good now."

Once you learn this process of going into theta and Commanding your good, miracles happen in many ways. Manifesting what you do want in your life becomes as natural as thinking a thing and having it be there. Every time you concentrate on what you wish to manifest, and then go to theta, it must manifest.

1. GROUND

The Earth is our provider. We are fueled and energized by the power of the magnetic forces of the Earth. The Earth gives us sustenance, through the food that we eat and the stability and foundation we rest upon, and in the powerful magnetic forces that radiate out to the edges of our atmosphere where they meet in equal measure the thermonuclear forces of the sun for our protection. The magnetic gravitational field of Earth is so strong that it stabilizes us in our Earth environment, yet it is so subtle that we walk, breathe, eat, and forget the magnetic power of the Earth that sustains us. When you are sending your energy down into the Earth, you are reconnecting to this amazing power and revitalizing all of your energy centers. A quick grounding any time of the day can stabilize you and harmonize your health, wealth, and sense of well-being. The first step in reaching out into a greater consciousness is to be well grounded in your physical consciousness. Imagine sending roots out from the bottom of your feet, going deep, deep down into the center of the force of the Earth, and imagine wrapping your roots around the element of gold or rubies and diamonds in large quantity in the center of Earth. Feel the power of your ground of being.

Three participants share their experience in grounding:

"Grounding to me is harmonizing my thoughts and harmonizing with the energy, the life force in all of creation. This goes down through the physical Earth and up, way beyond planet Earth. But as it does this, the energy that is me becomes refined and gets to where it is in sync with the other energy as opposed to being in opposition, which is something I have experienced in the physical body. The resonance between all of the power below and the power above turns into an expansion of all of life everywhere. It goes out a ways, beyond the galaxies. As it does, then my intention to be in harmony, to align with that energy, allows it to magnetize back to me, well grounded in the Earth. It is the harmony between my intention, and All of Everything that changes and stops the dissonance between what is over there and what is here so that they vibrate together, then it is all one."

"As an Earth child I am supposed to be grounded, but I haven't found that to be the case so in this first step I found that to be the strongest experience. I could feel my energy wrapping around the Earth. I felt like the Sherwin Williams paint ad wrapping around the globe and then my roots really went deep. This helped my energy flow and the rest of the process was easy. My ability was already there; I was just plugging in the parts. The confirmations that I got, the neatest part I heard was, 'We want you to have this.' Awesome."

"I was rockin'. I grounded and went up, and my whole body was just... I could hardly stand. I almost had to reach out and hold on to my partner. I thought I was just going to go right over. The second time, the expanded idea, was to pay it forward. Somebody is waiting to give to you, and somebody else is waiting to receive from you, and it just flows, just like that. "

2. ALIGN

Once you are well grounded, imagine the power and force of Earth's energy coming into your body, and align your heart to that force. As you take a breath in and then exhale, imagine your breath exhaling out in all directions around you as you clear negativity and align with love. You increase the power of your desires when they resonate in harmony, and you strengthen, like a lightening rod, the clarity of creating what you desire when you claim it in love.

3. GO TO THETA

Imagine a golden laser beam of light coming down into you from above, then going through you, and down below you into the Earth. Imagine the bolt of light as a constant, steady directional beam, one in which you can travel out into the outer regions of the galaxies and beyond. Imagine moving your consciousness up this beam of light, out through the top of your head, and travel out to the outer edges of the planet, travel on through the solar system, out through the Milky Way, out to the outer edges of the galaxy until you push through the black void of space into the white luminescence of Source. This is the place of creation of all that you desire. Practice thinking and feeling from this state of consciousness as you activate your wealth DNA in the cells of your body, your emotions, and your mind to be that master that you are.

A participant reports:

"When I am in theta, in the presence of the Creator and this amazing place of unconditional love and all the potential of all that is, I find it hard to return to ordinary life. This is that place of peace I have always longed for. I find that when I do return, I have that sense of peace and security within me for longer and longer periods of time. Eventually, I have noticed that it has become my natural way of viewing the world. What a change."

4. COMMAND

Now is the time to feel the emotions of your desire for that which you wish to manifest. Perhaps it is more money, paying off a bill, increasing your income, a new relationship, more love, a new car, more spiritual understanding, or a physical healing. Think upon that which you wish to manifest, and now, while in theta, silently and mentally Command: I don't know how (fill in the blank – for example, I have more money to pay my bills). I only know that I do now, and I am fulfilled!

Hold the thought of what you wish to manifest, imagine it while in theta, and Command that it is so! When you are creating in theta, you are bypassing your limited mind and your fearful thoughts.

Your Source Mind does know how to manifest anything that you desire, even when you don't. Always make your statements in the now! There is no future or "will" in your subconscious mind.

You are Commanding your subconscious mind, your DNA, and your Source Mind to operate in the now! Yes, it may take time to appear in physical form, but now is the only moment in consciousness that exists in creation.

When you state it as now, everything in you begins to search for the way to make that Command come true. Faith is Commanding and declaring your truth now, with trust that it is so. Command: I don't know how (I love myself). I only know that I do now, and I am fulfilled!

Remember that, every time you are thinking a fearful thought of loss or lack, you are thinking it now and perpetuating that as your reality. Training yourself to think your desirable future happens only by doing it now and declaring it is so in the now! Remove "will happen" from your vocabulary. Command: I don't know how (my beautiful future is mine now). I only know that it is now, and I am fulfilled*!*

5. EXPAND

While you remain in theta, you now apply one of the simplest, yet most powerful, techniques for manifesting good in your life as you imagine what it is that you desire in a bigger way, in a greater capacity, an expanded version that serves more good than your original idea. When you expand your idea to become something bigger than you, you increase its capacity to manifest.

This is the Law of Attraction in its highest form in action. Here you expand your idea of what it is you wish to manifest. Allow yourself to bring in an idea greater than you, an idea greater than your original thought. While in theta, allow your Source Mind to create even more for you than you can even imagine for yourself, more beauty and harmony in what you are manifesting, more grace and ease, a greater capacity; and allow your imagination to have this experience.

A participant shares her experience:

"I was surprised when I expanded my idea. My subconscious mind said, Here is our chance to ask, and it asked for something I didn't even know I wanted. It was really interesting when I thought, "No, that's too big." No, it's not too big. That changed, as there was this joy stepping on the paper and declaring I want to imagine that, and it even began to expand more. I could see more of the details of what that would be like, how the day started, and how it ended. Who was with me? The enjoyment I experienced (and there were different parts), that all of that information came very quickly into this picture, and that I was having all these separate experiences. . .and there were all these small moments of satisfaction knitted together that was part of this experience, this picture, this bigger thing that I knew I wanted. I thought that was my ego thinking this stuff, and I heard back, No, you are talking to God. It was wonderful."

6. RECEIVE WITH GRATITUDE

Now that you have experienced an idea greater than you and your manifestation has taken on its own form, its own life, you then receive this experience with gratitude. Move your consciousness back down the golden beam of light into your physical body and imagine the particles of consciousness of your manifestation floating down from Source into your body, into the cells of your body, and into your DNA itself. Imagine unwinding, unwinding, unwinding all the old limiting ideas and rewinding, rewinding, rewinding, a new holographic image of this life that is your new life replicating itself in every DNA strand in your body, in every organ of your body, in every hair follicle of your body, and in every particle of emotion in your body and your thinking. Feel it, accept it, and give thanks. Thank you! It is done! So be it!

Take a deep breath and send your energy down into the Earth to firmly re-establish your ground of being. Adjust your energy; let your body stretch, flex, and move with this new understanding of reality.

Come once again fully awake and alert into your body, open your eyes, and return to the room.

The summary of the Six-Step Process to go to theta and apply The One Command with a partner is found in the Appendix.

Chapter Eleven

Acting without Evidence

The demonstration of good that you are seeking arrives only by taking the first step of faith—action without evidence—by declaring that your greater intelligence provides all the good that you desire, and all the financial gain you wish to manifest.

We can only know what we are creating in our thinking when it manifests in physical reality. If you want to know what you are thinking, then simply look at your life now.

The life you have now has been created by your thinking. It is powerful and secure to know that as you have created this life that you have with your thoughts, you have the power to redirect your thinking and thereby manifest new realities of experience such as more money, wealth, grace, and ease.

In the same way that you are creating your life now, you can create a new, prosperous life with just a small shift in thinking, the active practice of going to theta, and applying The One Command daily.

This practice is what causes the shift in your wealth and money and your life. You must receive prosperity when you send the right messages to your Source Mind. It must manifest for you because what you are thinking now is manifesting for you.

Throughout this teaching, you are being shown how to disengage your thinking from what it is now and to connect to all the random potentiality of what is possible for you. A wonderful experience of who you are in the accomplishment of your dreams and desires is waiting for you with all the good you can possibly imagine as you learn what it feels like in your DNA itself to manifest from a conscious choice.

Success Story

One doctor of chiropractic was struggling financially with his business. He had clients who had not paid him for a very long time, and had large, outstanding debts. A few days after applying, The One Command, he was in his office and two clients who owed him a great deal of money came in and paid him all the money they owed. By applying The One Command, he had changed his thinking in such a way that he could receive payment and feel that he deserved to be paid. It was a fine demonstration of the power of his own thinking.

SECTION III
Your Greater Capacity

Chapter Twelve

The Power of Your Effect in the World

The power of your effect in the world as you shift your consciousness for good, increases your positive influence in quantum measure rather than in some small way. When you direct your life from that greater capacity within you or your Source Mind, through The One Command, you bring much good and abundance to those in your environment and your atmosphere. You bring good to your family and the world.

No effort is required to change any outside circumstance of your life when you change your inside understanding of the truth of who you are. When you think and feel in a state of love and gratitude with conviction and certainty, those in your immediate circle of influence, as well as those around the globe, feel that effect.

You are already masters of the life that you are creating, attracting to you the experiences that you unconsciously believe, and repelling from you any experiences that may rock the boat of those beliefs.

When your subconscious mind believes a certain way, it makes that a reality. This is how and why you are creating the life you have right now. If you think that it is hard to get cash, then a large pile of money, or even gold, could be sitting directly on your dining room table and you would say that is not yours, and you would walk around it or give it to someone else and make it disappear.

Or as many have experienced, when you receive some extra cash, immediately you have some disaster that removes that gain. You are not only attracting to you your experiences, you are also repelling, by your thinking, the very good that you are seeking.

Imagine a radio tower, one that is sending out radio waves in patterns of sound and information: dot, dot, dot, dash, dash, dash. This is an example of how you send your thoughts into the world, and how you receive thoughts from others, from the impulses of your thinking.

Your brain and your body send out into the world that state of consciousness that you believe internally, and your brain seeks only those experiences that verify your beliefs.

If you think that life is a struggle, or that there is never enough, or that others can have theirs but you can't, then that is what you attract. You attract those circumstances in a job, or the kind of people who verify that reality. This is not a chance occurrence. This is a determined outcome. It is the Law of Cause and Effect in action.

Your mind is doing the job it has been assigned—to attract only what you believe is possible, and to keep away any reality that contradicts those beliefs.

Once you come to know that you are the operator of your own reality equipment, you have the power to change your life by making new choices in your thinking.

Quantum Shifts

When you make a shift in your consciousness, it is a quantum curve. It is not linear. When you identify with prosperity, peace, and joy within you, you attract that experience in the world outside of you, and the fears of chaos or terrorism become a concept of possibility rather than a fact. When you are identified with that greater capacity within you, the capacity for diminishing violence in the world is increased as well.

In his book Power vs. Force, David Hawkins describes a model of Levels of Consciousness, ranging from zero to one thousand. The lower end of the scale, from zero to two hundred, contains the baser emotions such as shame, guilt, grief, fear, and anger. According to Hawkins, 85 percent of the world lives in this level of consciousness.

Above two hundred, we know courage, and have the first experience of our own power, rather than being oppressed by the force of others.

In our lower levels of consciousness, we operate within a state of duality in our thinking; we experience an either-or attitude of fear or anger, fight or flight, and we are highly influenced by outside beliefs and circumstances.

When you reach a level of consciousness above two hundred, you are operating in choice of your actions and thinking, and at five hundred, you are living as an awakened being, accepting yourself and others, and living in love and joy.

What is wonderful to know is that a small shift in you, in your level of consciousness, has a quantum effect in your world, and in the larger world.

Many of you are living on the planet at this time because you have a desire to be of service and to offer help in the world. It is wonderful to know that as you help yourself increase your capacity to prosper, and as you learn to love and live in joy, you are making that contribution to others by your simple efforts to change and improve your life. As you raise your consciousness in your thinking, a simple shift in you resonates that shift to millions.

You elevate their knowledge. You are not simply influencing those in your immediate circle; you are changing the fabric of space and thought. If something is known within you, then it exists and is known everywhere. If one good thing is known by you, it can be known by anyone.

Baseline of Our Thinking

We live in an agreed-upon reality of our collective intelligence that creates a baseline of thinking. When you change yourself, you change the world; you raise the baseline. You never need to think that you are not doing enough for others. When you are doing anything in a heightened state of realization and prosperity for yourself, you are helping millions of others to shift and to know it as well.

Chapter Thirteen

Unified Mind

When we seek a better experience in life, we want to transform ourselves mentally, emotionally, and energetically; we want to align the cells of our body into a unified state of thinking and being rather than living in an internal war. We seek a unified state where we are in a capacity of flow with our greater level of consciousness.

In the psychology of our emotions, when we expand our consciousness, we are including all of the various parts of love and fear. We are going to a point of balance within our selves into a higher level of consciousness. We are arriving at a state of non-judgment, of non-duality. You become you in a state of being.

Your state of being is different from your state of doing. It is a unified state of self in the pause of all that you are, without thought or judgment or knowledge of anything in your conscious brain, and with implicit trust in the understanding that a greater you holds you dear, sacred, and protected, and it looks out for your safety and best interests.

And this all occurs outside your range of ordinary thinking.

How can you make the shift from a state of fear-based duality that is affected by the outside influences of the world, into an expanded, internal, unified state in which you trust yourself and your decisions?

When you are a master of creating cash in your life, a master of creating money in your life, you become a master of creating everything in your life. It's the same principle.

You can create the right relationship because you can attract that right relationship. You use the same process to create an expansion of friendship. You use the same process to create a beautiful home for yourself. When you are connected to this unified state of who you are in consciousness of that greater capacity of yourself, you are remembering all of who you are. You are remembering all of that soul body of yours that lives eternally. You are remembering that part of you that is truly amazing. It's amazingly brilliant. It's amazingly fruitful. It's an amazingly loving being within you.

When you are operating with consciousness of this connection to your higher dimensional brain, you are in essence shifting out of the addictive patterns of your neural-net map that are attached to the lower levels of consciousness.

Live in Another Portion of Your Brain

A wonderful teacher, J. Z. Knight, who helped bring the movie What The Bleep Do You Know to the world and who has taught and channeled for almost thirty years, shared her experience with a women's group in Dallas, Texas.

She tells the story of how she had just come through a very debilitating illness that had affected her greatly. As she was suffering and in pain, the thought occurred to her in a moment, that of the six billion people on the planet, there were many who were well and who had an understanding of wellness in their bodies and their minds.

She also had the thought that there were billions of people who had lived healthy lives until they simply died of old age, and as a consequence of that knowledge, the knowledge of being well exists. The knowledge of being well and healthy exists. If the knowledge exists, then we may have that knowledge.

She knows that the brain has great unused portions and these unused portions are not programmed with any neuro-net pathways of any kind. There are only certain portions of the brain that are programmed with our beliefs, limited portions. We have an unlimited portion of our brain that's an available vessel for us to play in the delight of our neurology and in which we can create new thoughts and ideas. This is what the other 85 percent of the unused portions of our brain are for.

J. Z. Knight had the thought; "I'm going to Command that I go to a portion of my brain that knows how to be well, and I'm going to live there. That's where I'm going to live in my brain; that's where I'm going to live in my mind; that's where I'm going to live in my consciousness." And she did. And instantly all of her symptoms were gone. Instantly, she was no longer sick. It has been a few years since she made that choice, and she is still well to this day.

Just as J. Z. Knight is operating in a completely new section of her mind, a completely new section of her brain, we are here to do the same.

This is what mastery is. Mastery is coming to know those unused portions of your brain that are available right now to be programmed in any way you desire—to come to use those sections of your mind that are waiting and available for you to create a destiny for you in any way that you can imagine—a way that is not based on your early childhood programming, or the programming of other lifetimes, or the DNA of your genetic ancestors. In a way that is not based on those identities in your thinking. You can let those older programs gently dissolve and disappear.

And as you make a deeper and more profound connection with Source within you, as a daily practice, as an operation within yourself of creating your life from this place of mastery, creating your life from this place of unity, this place of potentiality, of non-knowledge, and not knowing, yet believing it is possible, then you must succeed.

Undo the Limits of Beloved Ego

If you are thinking, feeling, and knowing from your emotional body and your emotional brain, then you are thinking and feeling from your limitations. You are creating your life through the thinking and feelings that are identified with your ego.

You already are masters, creating every moment in your life. When you are shifting into a conscious awareness of an awakened awareness of your alignment with that greater capacity within you, you say, "Look at the delight of what is available, of the excitement, of the curiosity, of the imagination, of anything that I can create, and maybe something that I haven't even thought of that I can create, something beyond my capacity to imagine at this moment. I can create that as well."

It is consciousness. It is consciousness brought into a discrete particle of information that you have chosen to be your reality. You have chosen to say at this moment, "This is my reality; this is my consciousness; this is my thought."

You are not only going to shift your beliefs around the addictive patterns of your old thinking, you are awakening and learning to operate in new portions of your brain that have been designed for you to use. Why else are they there? Declare, "I want it!" And the more and more awakened you are, the greater use of your brain you have, the greater use of your mind you have, the greater use of your intelligence you have, the more prosperous and rich a life you can lead. . .easily and naturally.

SECTION IV
The One Command

Chapter Fourteen

The One Command - Part I

Apply The One Command in every situation until it is known in your body, your DNA, your emotions, and your brain.

The One Command arrived for me in that moment when I had to let go of all the ideas I had in my small, ordinary thinking mind, which I usually depended on to make my life work. I simply didn't have the answers for solving my seemingly insurmountable financial problems, and yet I was aware that there was some greater part of me that did.

I had been told many times that I was the only one standing in my way, and I understood what I was being told, but I didn't know how to change it. I often said that much of my good had come in spite of myself. I would dig in my heels and have to be dragged forward inch by inch, for my growth and my good, rather than taking the simple easy way I now know.

I wanted to "seemingly be in control." I was told many times, "Let go and let God" and I wanted to, yet at the same time there was a visceral clenching within me that still wanted to do it by my own thinking and reasoning.

When The One Command arrived, I was clear that I actually and literally didn't see any way out of my situation, except through great loss and defeat.

The old pattern I was so familiar with ran something like this:

Imagine the worst outcome of the situation and cry about it, then become even more worried to the point of nervous stress, lose my appetite, worry some more, become depressed, toss and turn in bed, and worry some more, and feel my body hurt; during this process create images and pictures, thoughts, words, and feelings that were the worst, most horrible, and devastating outcomes I could imagine. I could see myself homeless, my family angry and upset with me. I would judge myself as a failure, and then feel even more defeated, embarrassed, and ashamed.

I think it is safe to say that many of you have experienced similar scenarios.

Physical and Emotional Change

By stating The One Command, I literally changed my physical and emotional state, until one day I noticed that I had arrived at a place of receptivity and was open to ideas and solutions that were from that greater part of me, that, by the way, always has the answers to any of our supposedly insurmountable large or small problems. It simply does.

The change began when I was shown the simple statement—I DON'T KNOW HOW—that would short-circuit lack and every fearful negative thought in me as it occurred.

The statement "I DON'T KNOW HOW" stopped my negative thoughts and interrupted the old neurological addiction to worrying. I had been well trained to be a negative, fearful thinker early on in my life, and I was quite proficient at it, just as I imagine many of you are.

When you say "I DON'T KNOW HOW," many physical and emotional changes occur in your body. Your ego is used to being in charge and running your life. This is a different way of thinking and being.

I experienced various physical sensations when I made the statement "I DON'T KNOW HOW." There seemed to be an emptiness in my center, and I often had the feeling of a lurch, of my body shifting back and forth from one reality to another. The emptiness was the new sensation of being relaxed, rather than twisted and stressed. It was such a new feeling that I couldn't identify it at first.

As I Commanded, "I DON'T KNOW HOW," I was literally withdrawing my energy from all the fearful, negative thoughts. This was such a new experience to my brain, my body, and my nervous system that it didn't seem right, when in fact, it was so perfectly right.

You can compare this experience to carrying a fifty-pound rock around for years, until it becomes so natural everything in you has made the adjustment to carrying the fifty-pound rock. Then when you put the rock down, your body and your mind have to adjust to walking without the rock. At first, your old point of reference is missing, and everything in you has to keep adjusting, until your new balance is established.

Ask for It to Be Different

When we ask for our life to be different, to have new experiences of wealth and prosperity the easy way, and to be rich with grace and ease, and we haven't had that yet, our body, mind, and emotions have no concept of what that would look, feel, taste, or smell like.

When we stop our old, negative thinking, the same is true. We have no concept of what life without that prattle could be. The negative thoughts and limiting ideas we have are there because we were trained to have them, and they serve a purpose in keeping each one of us safe in the world according to that training.

When you are asking for an improvement in your life—a change of circumstances, more income, or better relationships—deep-seated, old beliefs have to change. The outer circumstances of our lives never vary until we have a new understanding within us to resonate to that level of living and being.

One Woman's Story

One woman had been living an apparently successful life with a good career and a grown daughter, yet she felt isolated and alone. She thought that unless she took care of her family and friends, they wouldn't want her, and there would be no good purpose for her in their lives. This was a deep-seated emotional block that had caused her pain all her life.

She began to Command, I don't know how I am valuable as myself with family and friends. I only know that I am now, and I am fulfilled.

Her mother, who seemed to call only when she wanted a favor or some help, called one day soon after this woman had started Commanding her good and spoke to her with genuine love, maybe for the first time ever. She said that she was calling because her daughter had been on her mind and she just wanted to tell her "I love you."

Since that day, new friendships and supportive relationship are normal for the woman. She unwound her belief that her only value was in what she did, not in who she was.

Chapter Fifteen

I Don't Know How

O nce you understand that, in truth, you don't know how, a greater good than you can imagine is on its way; it is easy to say, "I don't know how."

Once you have an idea of what you want to create or eliminate in your life, then let go and stop figuring it out by saying, *"I don't know how."*

There is a much greater capacity within you, with more intelligence and power than what you know in your simple little brain, and no matter how smart or intelligent you are, it is only a small, partial expression of your true intelligence.

You are turning over the how to that greater intelligence of you, who will bring you a much greater amount of good than what you ask. You'll find a better solution, and will do it with greater refinement and synchronicity than you could ever design or create with your small mind.

The easy way to make that change is to first STOP your old pattern of thoughts and float in the UNKNOWN for a while.

The P A U S E is necessary to let that
***greater part of you* communicate with you**
BY SAYING
I DON'T KNOW HOW!

Tune into Your Greater Good

That greater part of you is you in the completion of who you are. It is the you who can, and does, have the ability to steer your course to achieve your dreams and desires. What is required is for that lesser part of you—your negative, fearful, limited self—to become quiet and still so that greater part can give you the gold it has for you.

The process of going to that greater capacity within you is so easy and the results so profound and magical, that you have to train your ego, your identity, and your thoughts and emotions to enjoy living this way.

There does come a time, after sufficient practice in using The One Command, when you know without evidence that your good is assured. There comes a time when you have a desire, you state The One Command, and what you ask for arrives. It arrives with no effort on your part. It arrives almost so easily that you can think that you are magical, because, by the way, you are!

Success Story

One day I was at home thinking about my father and how much I respected him for all that he accomplished before his death. At the same time I was thinking about the fear and negativity he gave to me because he had lived through the Great Depression. Even as he succeeded, there was an undertone of fear that his success might be taken away or lost.

I wanted to create another level of success for myself, and I was investigating what limiting beliefs I could still be holding in my unconscious data banks. I knew that my father was my model for how I worked and earned a living in the world, and there were still some deeper unconscious issues that I couldn't quite get to about my dad's fearful thinking.

I went into theta and began saying The One Command: I don't know how I clear my father's limiting money and security beliefs from me now. I only know that I do, and I am fulfilled.

I was simply musing with this statement for a day or two, and then I got a phone call. A gentleman called me and said that he had met my chiropractor who told him about me, and then he had gone to my Web site and upon seeing my photo, he knew that we had to meet. He was interested in theta and wanted to know if he could come to my home right away. We set up a time, and the next day he arrived at my front door. I had no real idea why he was coming to my home, but the energy of the phone conversation was very positive, and I looked forward to our meeting.

After an hour or so of conversation out on the patio, during which we talked about the teaching I was doing and his interest in my work, he said, "I also have some techniques that I use for clearing old beliefs, and I would like to share them with you. Do you have anything that you would like to clear up?"

It was a bit awkward at first, but then I thought, "Well, why not?" I began to share, and I talked about my dad and some of his ideas that I thought could be in the way of a greater success in my life.

I then went through the Six Steps and Commanded a change in the underlying beliefs that rose to the surface, beliefs that were exactly on point as to the limiting money and security ideas my dad had given me.

He then left, and I have never heard from him again.

The next month, my income quadrupled.

Imagine that: good came right to my door.

Chapter Sixteen

You Know What You Think by Your Results

When you apply The One Command, you are sending a resonance out into the universe where like-minded individuals can and will respond. When you ask for more cash or an improvement in your living circumstances or better relationships, they arrive in many different ways.

The requirement to stay in the process
is to have faith.
Faith is trust, without evidence, that the process works....

Eventually, you begin to see intuitively the dynamics behind the curtain, preparing to bring you your good. When I Command the next good thing in my life, now I KNOW without doubt that it will arrive.

It must arrive because it is the Law of Attraction in action, and my only requirement is to be prepared to receive my good. Your only requirement is to be prepared to receive your good.

As you operate in states of awareness beyond your conscious ability to know your thoughts, the only way that you can experience you is by the results of your life.

You can know your thinking by the events that take place in your life. When you demonstrate over and over the fruits of your thinking in a positive manner, with good results, then you can know that you have shifted old, negative, limiting ideas about yourself. If you want more than you have, then you simply ask for the knowledge to clear whatever is in the way, so that you can have more.

When you create a pause between thoughts, or stop some limited idea, then that greater capacity of who you are can manifest your greater desire that you also hold, but have not experienced yet.

The Law of Free Will Choice allows only that which you state unconsciously and consciously as your truth, to be manifested back to you as your life experience.

When you send your thoughts into the universe, throughout all dimensions of self and your Source Mind, what you receive back is you responding to you. That is you! That is you in the capacity of your intelligence of who you are. It is the availability of your intelligence connecting to the potentiality of All That Is, in your act of creation.

Success Story

This story begins with an inventor and his wife. One day the inventor put his mind to harnessing electronic electroluminescent (EL) lighting as an alternative to toxic snap chemical lights often used for automobile accident flares.

After patenting his idea, he and his wife formed a company to begin the production and manufacture of the battery-operated substitute lighting source. The stress was high, and he began to suffer some heart problems from the business of implementing his dream. At one point, he and his wife even considered abandoning the whole project because they had gone so deeply in debt and were on the edge of financial collapse.

I met with them, and in our first meetings, both he and his wife began to engage in the theta brain wave as a technique to stop fear and allow success. After a few sessions clearing fearful negative beliefs, he noticed that his heart problem improved and eventually disappeared.

In addition to the financial stress, the young man had been raised in a very negative environment. In fact, his father, who was quite skilled himself, was working with him in the business, but it was a push-pull emotional roller coaster. Dad did help in the physical work, but along with the help, he gave his son a daily dose of fearful thinking and negativity, repeatedly saying that the product wouldn't work and his son would fail.

Again, the young man went into that greater capacity within himself and continued to stop and change every limiting idea and belief that caused him distress, including his father's negative proclamations.

Through persistence and focus on an idea greater than he had even originally imagined, he and his wife achieved great success, and today their company is valued over 4.5 million dollars.

They know the quality of their thinking by the results they achieved!

Chapter Seventeen

The One Command - Part II

I only know that I do now, and I am fulfilled!
I only know that I am now, and I am fulfilled!
I only know that it is so now, and I am fulfilled!

The second part of The One Command—I only know that I do now, and I am fulfilled—is literally commanding your subconscious mind, conscious mind, and your Source Mind to bring that reality into your life. That is the action of faith.

I don't know how **(fill in the blank, for example: I pay my bills quickly and easily).** *I only know that I do now, and I am fulfilled.*

The One Command is different than anything you have been taught before. It is completely different than affirmations, and different than setting an intention, creating an exact model of what you want, or a vision board. Those are all useful for creating the energy of what you desire and for your dream, but The One Command is 100 percent effective in manifesting it.

How many of you have had or now have affirmations pasted all around your home and office, from bathroom mirror to computer? Affirmations such as:

I love myself
I love myself
I AM
I AM
My financial good is on its way
Divine right money comes to me now
I am blessed
It is mine

Many of you have practiced long lists of affirmations, hundreds of affirmations, and still haven't manifested more money, or a better relationship, or peace of mind. Affirmations are good and beneficial in a limited way. They are a support system to retrain your brain and your subconscious mind. In this teaching, you are simply going to change the programming that disallows you to have it instantly, and to become 100 percent effective in manifesting your desires.

The One Command is one Command that can be used in any situation!

While you are in your Source Mind, and you issue The One Command, you stop your little self from going forward with its limited ideas. You are you, creating you. I am going to say it again. You are you, creating you and the life that you desire.

You have a thought and a desire of something that you want or something that you believe, and as you emotionally place your attention on those thoughts, they activate all of your body, mind, and spirit to be in compliance.

Energetically, at all times, you are thinking unconscious thoughts that are driving your wants and needs. Your thinking continues while awake or asleep. A belief is an idea about you and others, and about the world that creates the lens of your focus.

If you are thinking a limiting thought, then that is the only thought that may be made manifest as a reflection of you. If you are focused on a greater idea, then that idea must manifest instead.

When you have a thought, limited or expansive, and the desire for some good, or a fear of something bad, you are radiating that thought out into all dimensions of your being and in consciousness to the world. When you are radiating your thoughts with your emotional feelings about what you desire or fear, then those emotional thoughts reach every level of your being, from the DNA to your Source Mind.

What You Send Out Is Returned to You

What you send out in consciousness can only be returned to you in experience because of the Law of Free Will Choice. There is no outside force overriding your desires. There is no obstructionist God preventing you from your good. There is only you in your capacity of your intelligence of who you are, connecting with the potentiality of All That Is.

You create limitation or success in your life by the thoughts you send into the world in the emotion of your thinking. If you send a thought (such as I desire to make more cash in my life; I desire to make more money than my expenses; I desire to be healthy; I desire to have a more loving relationship; I desire to have a better body), and at the same time you are unconsciously feeling I don't deserve, then all messages are emanating out in consciousness. You are sending out the duality of I don't deserve—I desire, and these thoughts are conflicting with each other. Your mental idea of what you desire has less power than your emotional idea of what you feel is true about yourself. How do you get past that?

You Apply The One Command and Resolve the Conflict.

You ask to quiet your fearful, limiting thoughts and create a p a u s e in your thinking by the simple statement I don't know how I deserve to have all that I desire. I only know that I do now, and I am fulfilled. You Command it. That is the only requirement.

You get clear on what you want. I don't know how to move out of my atmosphere of poverty. I only know that I do now, and I am fulfilled. I don't know how I get out of my atmosphere of lack. I only know that I do now, and I am fulfilled.

When you are in that space of I don't know how, you quiet your entire negative, limiting ideas and beliefs. You stop your repetitious mantra of lack. You quiet your mind, your emotions, and your thinking—everything. Everything quiets.

And then when you say, "*I only know I do now, and I am fulfilled,*" your creative self says, "Let's find an amazing solution," or, "Let's bring lots of cash into your life right now. Let's get busy; we have a new direction to follow."

Every part of you is excited to have carte blanche to bring you a pair of thoroughbreds instead of a broken-down horse.

This is different than what you have been taught is possible, as you take what you desire to theta, Command it, increase it in a greater capacity than what you originally thought, and experience it energetically, returned to you in gratitude.

Chapter Eighteen

Expectancy

Y ou may notice that what you are learning is different than any other teaching on manifesting that you have ever heard. You are learning the higher principles behind the ideas in affirmations, or vision mapping, or writing out a complete and specific description of what you wish to manifest.

All those tools are useful for you in your beta thinking brain to clarify your desire of knowing what experience that you wish to create.

If you do not know the experience that you wish to create, then your Source Mind and the universe cannot manifest it for you. However, you can Command that understanding. The One Command is designed to answer each and every fear, confusion, or doubt you may have.

You can simply state, I don't know how my vision for my life is made clear to me. I only know that it is now, and I am fulfilled.

Once you have the design of prosperity that you wish to create as your new future, or the nature of a new relationship, or good health, the next step is to let it arrive with the expectancy of success by letting it go and sending it to the universe via The One Command.

FIRST FOLLOW THE STEPS UP TO SOURCE
GROUND, ALIGN, GO TO THETA

AND THEN COMMAND

I DON'T KNOW HOW (FILL IN THE BLANK WITH WHAT YOU DESIRE; FOR EXAMPLE: I INCREASE MY INCOME).

I ONLY KNOW THAT I DO NOW, AND I AM FULFILLED.

EXPAND INTO YOUR GREATER CAPACITY, AND RECEIVE IN YOUR DNA, UNWIND AND REWIND WITH GRATITUDE.

Pull Your Future Toward You

You have many probable futures, and where you concentrate your thoughts in a certain direction, that is the future you are pulling towards you. To increase your good, you must let go of how the form of that future will arrive.

In your small-thinking and problem-solving capacity of beta, you limit the information that you can receive from sources beyond your own model of reality.

You are training yourself to not know the form of your good, because the design and blueprint that you can imagine consciously are only a small particle of your unlimited consciousness that you cannot know with your brain. Later on, you use that wonderful beta mind to take the action steps necessary for the implementation of your good.

It Is a Process

When you first discover the feeling of expectancy of cash and your financial good arriving without knowing how, your body, mind, and emotions have to adjust to your new position in the universe.

Upon receiving demonstration after demonstration of the proof of this process of your financial good arriving, you develop a physical sensor, and a feeling of that good about to arrive. That wonderful feeling is addictive.

Next, this process of manifesting cash and good in your life becomes natural. Your ego says, "Okay, I get it; I just didn't understand at first how well this works."

Chapter Nineteen

The One Command - Part III

It is not enough to stop old thoughts and fears about money. It is even more important to generate new information within your DNA and the cells of your body, to receive and accept your new financial good.

The third part of The One Command, "I am fulfilled," is your gratitude and your blessing that it is so. It is the way to permanently rearrange the energy of your old thinking in your data banks.

Your gratitude and blessing of your prosperous new circumstances have great power in bringing happiness, satisfaction, and joy, along with your riches.

As you know what you know now without thinking about it, what you are creating now by The One Command becomes your new subconscious beliefs, your new emotional beliefs about money, happiness, and satisfaction, and your new emotional identity about being rich and prosperous.

For example, you don't have to remind yourself to worry about money, do you? You notice that those thoughts simply arise on their own in your mind, and you have concentrated on those thoughts until you were super concentrated with worry. You know how to worry without thinking.

You are now training yourself to know how to be financially secure and prosperous in your thinking, and to know what it feels like to have all the money that you desire—in the same manner, without having to remember to think about it.

The old-fashioned, difficult way was to force yourself to change.

The new, easy way is to experience the prosperous truth of finances and money within you, and the world will act accordingly. It must.

The turnaround is to place the power of your spoken words and thoughts into creating a money flow. When you do this by going to Source and Commanding your financial good, a direct link is established between your emotions, your brain, and your DNA, and you create new neuro-pathways for cash to arrive instantly in your life.

When your old way of thinking arises in your brain with limiting, fearful money thoughts, The One Command is your Command tool to stop the negativity of your old thinking by saying:

I DON'T KNOW HOW

When you think a thought of lack or of fear, or if you find yourself talking poor talk, stop yourself by quickly going to Source and stating the real truth:

**I don't know how my financial good comes to me now.
I only know that it does, and I am fulfilled!**

See how quickly money comes. It shows up in the mail, from people who owe you money, from bonuses, or in the form of more clients or work, and in unexpected ways.

This simple statement is so powerful that you will experience physical reactions to the neurological changes in your brain.

You are giving up old, addictive thinking patterns that are harming you, and you are retraining your brain and body for the good you have always wanted every time you engage The One Command.

You are training yourself through breath, through trust, to let yourself change into this new pattern. Soon enough, it will become your new, natural way of thinking.

Success Story

One gentleman learned about The One Command from his wife. He ran his own welding business and had no clients lined up for any work. His wife, who was attending a Commanding Wealth® course, said as he didn't have any jobs, he didn't have any excuse for not attending, so he might as well come along.

He wasn't quite sure what to expect, but he participated and came to an "Aha!" understanding as he embraced this new knowledge. He sincerely Commanded for new work by going to theta and stating, "I don't know how new jobs are mine now. I only know they are, and I am fulfilled."

On Sunday evening, when he returned home, his answering machine was completely filled with job requests. He took time off on Monday to go through the requests, practicing one of the fundamental notions of this teaching that we want to do it "the easy way," and selected the right company for him.

Because it was a large oil rig construction company that had their own equipment, he didn't have to haul his welding equipment on and off his truck, which is hard labor. He was hired as an independent contractor, and he received twice the salary he could have earned as a full-time employee.

He, his wife, and their children have enjoyed trips around the world, reduced their debt, increased their savings, and improved his health by simply Commanding his good.

SECTION V
The Practice

Chapter Twenty

Focus On Your Desire

S tart with a thought. Every master of wealth starts with the thought of what she or he wishes to accomplish. When you realize that you shape reality rather than conform to outside circumstances, you begin to live a magical and rich life.

The One Command is amazingly easy and simple to apply because it is not similar to an affirmation that you must repeat for results. It is a live energy that arrives out of the moment of a thought.

When you are thinking of something good and a negative or fearful thought arises, you simply meet it by going to theta and making The One Command.

I discovered that the easy way to accomplish your financial and emotional goals is to operate from that greater capacity that knows and holds a truth for you, even when you forget to hold that truth for yourself.

When we focus on the desire of our greater truth, that greater truth is what we come to manifest and create.

The Cause of Lack

Many have come into an acceptance of powerlessness over their destinies. This powerlessness is based on what was learned in childhood—the decisions we made about feeling safe, or unsafe in the past, and our unconscious acceptance of what others tell us is or is not possible in the present.

We often do not have what we want, not because of our inability or capability, but simply because we have been trained not to. We have been trained not to have what we want by those in our environment who have told us of our limitations. We have been trained to be fearful; we have been trained to doubt ourselves.

We have been trained by discouraging ideas, and by hearing how difficult the world is. We have been trained to feel that it is impossible to achieve our desires.

Our desires remind us to be steadfast to the truth of what we can have, and in the moment of opposition, we apply The One Command to retrain our brains, our emotions, and our bodies to stay steadfast to their importance.

Commanding a Home

One newly divorced woman who wanted to buy her own home was told she couldn't qualify for a loan because her husband had declared bankruptcy before their recent divorce. In addition, she had spent only a few months in her first job ever, and she had no established credit. She was told that she shouldn't even think about owning her own home.

Many people she talked to, including representatives of mortgage companies and real estate offices, said the same thing: "You just went through a divorce, you are newly in a job for the very first time, you have no credit history, and you have a bankruptcy in your past. It is impossible. You simply won't qualify for buying a home."

This is an example of what many would say is "the reality of the situation." This is how the world works. You don't fit the criteria for home ownership. It is out of the question.

However, this is not "the reality" of the situation, because we are creating our own reality. It is instead a description of standards and practices in the world. It is not reality unless you surrender to that limitation.

In reaction to being told that she couldn't qualify to own a home, she might have said, "I may as well not even have the desire to own my own home because I can't. I have been told I can't, and that is the end of it."

However, a master of wealth would have a completely different attitude, one that this beautiful woman had.

Recognize and Honor Your Desire

It began with her recognizing and honoring the desire to own her own home. Let us imagine that desire was only as far as she could go in manifesting what she wanted.

If the woman believed what the outside world told her, then she would have been defeated in her desire. She would have been defeated in just the desire, I want a home, and she would have said, That is an impossible idea; I can't have a home.

The way we create our preferred reality and become the authors of our own script is by staying true to the essential intrinsic power of our desire. Even when we hear others who are negative about what is possible for us, we go to theta and simply issue The One Command: "I don't know how I own my own home. I only know that I do now, and I am fulfilled."

Rather than having doubts so grave that they affect your focus to such an extent that you give up your essential desire, which is that dream within you that you wish to fulfill, you say in that moment, "I don't know how I fulfill my dream. I only know that I do now, and I am fulfilled."

In other words, if you are told that you can't, or are told that you have to "get real" and see reality as blocks put in place by standards and practices, then even if you accept that, you have not been told that you can't still have a dream of that desire.

It is known that standards and practices in lending money or home ownership are very different today than they were only a few years ago. If you surrender your dream, when it is not in agreement with the outer operations of the world, you forget the very essence of the attitude of wealth, and that essence says that every good we desire starts with a thought.

Rather than surrender to the standards and practices of the moment, because that is all they are—rules that change often and rapidly in any given culture—we can elevate our thinking to another outcome, one in which we attain our desires.

This woman kept her desire. She kept the dream by recognizing and honoring the desire to own her own home and continued saying, I don't know how, because she didn't. In issuing that One Command of her desire, her mind, emotions, and greater intelligence immediately sought to find an answer.

She held to her dream as she stated The One Command: "I don't know how I buy a home. I only know that I do now, and I am fulfilled" and sent out to the universe her desire of this greater truth.

The universe can only respond to the truth to which we give power. We are all masters with the ability to create our lives. We are creating our lives right now.

The woman had the thought that she wanted to own her own home and was told that it was impossible, yet she was steadfast and true to her desire of I want to own my own home.

When a negative idea, such as "I can't own my own home,"

showed up, she redirected her energy by the simple Command, I don't know how I own my own home. I only know that I do now, and I am fulfilled.

While simply holding that thought, she went about her daily business, in grace and confidence, and with ease. The pleasure of the thought itself, I own my own home, began to engage her and she would sometimes chuckle at that thought.

She was also putting "down payment" money away in a special savings account in anticipation of owning her own home. If a limiting, negative thought intruded, she answered it calmly by going into theta and stating The One Command, "I don't know how I own my own home. I only know that I do now, and I am fulfilled."

She had been saving for some months, and had a nice down payment fund, when a friend invited her to go for a drive in the country on the weekend. When they got together for their small road trip, they talked and caught up on each other's lives, and during the conversation, the woman shared her dream of owning a home.

Her friend exclaimed, "Why, I heard about a new town house development just a few miles from here. Let's go check it out."

The town homes were delightful and had all the aspects that the woman had imagined: large, sunny rooms, trees all around, good shopping within an easy drive, and an affordable price.

Dare she to imagine one of these beautiful homes as hers? With confidence, she approached the staff with an offer to purchase a home, and quickly explained her circumstances: new job, recent divorce, and a bankruptcy. She told them she did have a $5,000 down payment, and could easily pay the mortgage.

Within hours after she returned home, she got the call that she had been approved to purchase the home, and she was ecstatic.

To this day, she still doesn't know how or why she was approved, only that she was, and she thoroughly enjoys living in her new circumstances.

Chapter Twenty-One

Command Your Prosperity

Taking the same amount of energy that you use worrying about lack and applying it to manifesting a new reality is so simple.

Redirecting your thinking to prosperity tunes you into your God/Source of all that is, that field of all possibilities, and provides you with all the financial good you can imagine and more, as you train your brain to receive that good.

God/Source and cash talk to each other all the time. Cash says, "Hey, Great Creator, you know I enjoy being appreciated, and I like to be with those folks that like me, want me, and think that it is a good, deserving thing to have me in their life; I'd like to be a blessing for them. Do you have anyone lined up?"

As you attend to attuning yourself to Source and to personalizing your wealth in your thinking, it is yours to have as a blessing in a never-ending, always-present flow of cash and financial good.

THE ONE COMMAND IS YOUR CAPACITY

Follow the Six-Step Process; go to theta and Command,
I don't know how my financial good comes to me now.
I only know that it does, and I am fulfilled!

Replace every fearful thought, and state every new desire in this simple statement, and as you put your brain into neutral, you will experience new ways of knowing and thinking about financial greatness and good beyond what you can even imagine!

You are Commanding your subconscious mind and your Source Mind to provide your financial good. You are replacing the thoughts of lack and fear with opportunity and riches.

New Programs of Wealth

You program your subconscious mind to go into theta, and through The One Command, you shift to another portion of your brain, that unused portion that's available for new ideas of reality.

You may find that this process is uncomfortable physically. It's uncomfortable physically because your old, subconscious survival programming is saying, "I don't know how to do that, and I don't believe it's true." But do it anyway.

Imagine reprogramming some of your fears and beliefs. Go to *theta* in the Six Steps mentally: Ground, Align, Go to *theta*, Command, Increase that to a greater idea, Receive with gratitude.

Start with, I don't know how _____. I only know it is so now, and I am fulfilled.

Try some of these beliefs.

I don't know how money is clean and pretty.
I only know it is so now, and I am fulfilled.

I don't know how money is free with no attachments.
I only know it is so now, and I am fulfilled.

I don't know how rich people are spiritual and compassionate.
I only know it is so now, and I am fulfilled.

I don't know how rich people are ordinary and normal.
I only know it is so now, and I am fulfilled.

I don't know how it is easy to be rich and wealthy.
I only know it is so now, and I am fulfilled.

I don't know how I pay my rent or mortgage.
I only know I do now, and I am fulfilled!

I don't know how I reduce my debt to zero.
I only know I do now, and I am fulfilled!

I don't know how I increase my income to ($XX amount) a month.
I only know I do now, and I am fulfilled!

I don't know how I drive a beautiful car that is paid for.
I only know I do now, and I am fulfilled!

I don't know how I have more clients.
I only know I do now, and I am fulfilled!

I don't know how I get a better job.
I only know I do now, and I am fulfilled!

I don't know how I own my own home.
I only know I do now, and I am fulfilled!

I don't know how I have great health.
I only know I do now, and I am fulfilled!

I don't know how I have the best relationships.
I only know I do now, and I am fulfilled!

I don't know how I am peaceful and calm when I ask for money.
I only know I am now, and I am fulfilled.

You Fill in The Blanks.

I don't know how I _____ .
I only know it is so now, and I am fulfilled.

I don't know how I _____ .
I only know I do now. I am fulfilled.

I don't know how I have _____ .
I only know I have it now, and I am fulfilled.

All the Evidence You Need

Your subconscious mind now has a new program. As you state The One Command, you are reprogramming your subconscious mind, and your subconscious mind in alignment with your Source mind is making this manifest.

It is your new reality.

It must manifest, just as your programming that you have now manifests, and it is outside of your awareness of your consciousness in your human body with your beta brain to understand how it does.

You cannot know.

That's why faith is required; it is the step between desire and manifestation. The step in faith in not knowing how, yet trusting that what you're creating is manifested.

You have all the evidence that your thinking is creating what you're manifesting now. Why doubt that your new thinking is going to create a new reality? It must; it simply must. It's the same principle of universal law in action.

Demonstration: An Increase of Income

An attractive and charismatic woman had a dream of being self-employed and financially independent. For years, she made an effort to get her own business going. She was, in essence, working two jobs—the one she got a salary for and the business she was building. Even with much dedication and persistence, too many fears and not enough income prevented her from leaving her day job.

She started Commanding a different outcome: I don't know how my business grows in income and relationships. I only know that it does now, and I am fulfilled. She concentrated on being in the place of not knowing how her financial good would arrive and yet knowing that it would.

Shortly after she began to Command her good to arrive, she began to see increases in appointments and requests for her services, until she recognized that, from her own talents, she had earned more in the last few months from her independent business than she had from her job.

With that demonstration of success, she went for it, quit her job, and launched her career. The very first month on her own, she continued to Command her financial good and tripled her income, earning more than she had ever made previously. She was elated and continues today with great success in her business.

Chapter Twenty-Two

Practice Does Make Perfect

hen you wonder if your are going to get that job or that raise or success in your business, you go to theta and Command, I don't know how I get that job, that raise, that success in my business. I only know I do now, and I am fulfilled. Thank you. I am fulfilled.

Any time you get a fear-based thought, say, just walking down the street, you go to theta and Command, I don't know how. I only know that it is so now, and I am fulfilled. Thank you.

The One Command *short-shifts* your neural-net pathways to reprogram your thinking into manifesting a new reality in that moment.

Are you understanding that?

When you focus on what you want, you manifest what you want. When you focus on your fear, when you focus on the bills in the drawer, you get bills because you're focused there. You get anxiety, stress, and feelings of separation and powerlessness when you focus there.

You're responsible to your bills. You're responsible to your debt. You're responsible for having income and a source of supply in cash or trade.

But when you're focusing on, "Oh my God, how can I pay my bills?" or when you're just quietly anxious over it, then what you are telling yourself is that there isn't enough, or there is no answer.

You stop that behavior by going into theta and Commanding, I don't know how I have all the money I need, peacefully and easily, to pay my bills. I only know I do now, and I am fulfilled.

Attracting Your Good

You don't know how, but you are now making a new Command to your subconscious mind, and your new programming will be acted upon. It must.

It will start sorting your reality to bring you the answer. It will sort your reality to bring you the people. It will sort your reality to magnetize to you the new experience of easy cash, of the boss that says yes. All the things that you're afraid you can't have, you change with The One Command: "I don't know how. I only know that I do now, and I am fulfilled."

And you stay in that energy. You stay focused in that energy. You train yourself in a new way. You have been trained to be afraid; you have been trained to doubt. You have been trained to feel less than you are. And this is a simple training with a simple statement.

Play with it. Get into it. Feel it.

It's not familiar to you.
This is something new you're learning.
You are retraining yourself.
This is the training of the masters of the world.

Richard Branson, one of the richest people in the world, is an exciting human being, a wonderful human being, compassionate; he invites people to play in his life.

He didn't know that he couldn't, so he just went and did.

And he did it again and again.

He might say, "You know, I did that. I have Virgin Records. I have all these smash people who became stars. I think I'll own an airline. That sounds great. Okay, that's a smash hit. I think I'll take a balloon ride across the world. Yeah, that's cool. I'll do a reality show. All right, why not? I'll get a supersonic jet that goes out of the atmosphere and go for a trip to the moon. Great—why not? You get to play in any dimension."

While in theta you Command,

I don't know how.

I only know that I do now, and I am fulfilled!

You have to let go, not focus on what you're afraid of. Not focus on the negative, not focus on what you are worried about, the bad news you are creating. You can refocus in a loving, gentle, kind, wonderful, spiritual, magnificent way, in an easy way.

It is the easy way!

I had been Commanding help to get this beautiful book written, and a few days after I began, I was talking to a participant in a course and I mentioned to her I was looking for someone to transcribe my tapes and help me with my book. We were having this conversation, and she said,

"I could bring my computer tomorrow, as I'm really fast at typing, and I could transcribe your tapes." And she did. Yes, thank you. It is that simple.

I don't know how to manifest clients, to manifest relationships. . . Go up into theta: I don't know how. I only know that. . . and just feel that transmission coming down, and I am fulfilled.

And when you say The One Command, and you are in programs that you are so addicted to—of the old way of thinking of not having it—you physically create a vacancy in your body.

You have this space of the ego dissolving and not knowing who you are in that moment. That's how powerful this is. It is you dissolving your old ego in one moment of letting go, of not knowing.

Process: Imagine

Take a minute to relax while you read the following. Ground and expand your energy. Loosely relax and read as if you were rocking in a boat on the water at the same time.

Now imagine that something mysterious has happened and you have an endless supply of money. Imagine having an endless supply of money. Can you even picture having all the money you can ever imagine? Millions, billions, trillions—an endless supply that replenishes immediately when you spend it. Everything you could ever want or need in cash is yours. There is an endless supply of cash in your life. Endless. There is an endless supply. What can you give yourself, allow yourself to have, with this endless supply? There is an endless supply of money—millions and billions of dollars for you. There is an endless supply. What can you give yourself in your life? What can you imagine giving yourself and having? How would you be? Imagine how would you be. Who are you? Who would you be? What do you look like? How do you dress? Can you give yourself a $5,000 outfit, a $100,000 wardrobe, millions of dollars worth of jewelry, just for the heck of it, just because you can? After you share it with all the people you want to share it with, help all the people you want to help, how are you helping your life? What can you give yourself? Can you give yourself more than one vehicle to drive? How about a chauffeur?

Can you give yourself somebody to drive you around? How about gardeners or housekeepers or cooks, private masseurs or personal trainers, private assistants, wardrobe assistants, what else? Who is there with you sharing in all that? You can spend an endless supply to feed the world, start up a bank and lend to anyone you want to, buy a country, fly to outer space, colonize a planet, you have an endless supply. An endless supply of cash is constantly available. It can never run out. How about an airplane? Want a little, you know, Lear jet? They're only $45,000,000. How about your own island? Who is enjoying it with you? What's your environment like? What kind of home or homes do you have? Can you imagine having more than one home: a home on the ocean, a home in the mountains, a home on other continents? And what are you doing in the world now that you already have all the money that you would ever need—it is already yours. What are you doing in the world? Who are you now that you have all the money—an endless supply of money? Who are you? Is your identity about needing to struggle to get the money, and you don't know who you are now that you have it? Or do you know who you are when you have all the money? What else would you like to do? Use your imagination. How much can you imagine is possible? How many people are you loving, laughing with, playing with? What kinds of pets do you have—a menagerie? What's your life like, as you have all the money—an endless supply? You can have that, too. You have an endless supply. There is no limitation on what you can have, and you have an endless supply of all the cash you could ever want and need. Whenever you want it, it's there. So simply say to yourself: I agree, I enjoy, thank you.

Now take a moment and close your eyes and imagine that as a possibility.

Was that easy or difficult? Did you limit yourself, tell yourself you shouldn't, couldn't, wouldn't? Or did you go for it?

SECTION VI
Qualities of Thought

Chapter Twenty-Three

An Original Thought

One day as I lowered my brain wave to theta, traveled through the Six-Step Process to my Source Mind, and Commanded my wealth, I was thinking about everything I had ever been told or learned from others, and I had the spontaneous notion that I would like to have a thought I had never had before.

I would like to have an original thought, one that hadn't been told to me. I would like to have a thought that I hadn't read. I would like to have a thought that was an original thought that came from some greater intelligence than my limited mind. I was rather pleased that I had even had the notion and the gumption to think I could have an original thought. Because what we concentrate on becomes real. Since that moment, I have been given a quantity of original thoughts. They have become this teaching. I think that as we grow here together, you will also find it enjoyable to ask for an original thought.

One woman, upon hearing the notion that we could ask for an original thought, has since written a book of poetry that has been published, and she is now working on two patents for inventions that were shown to her.

Another gentleman is developing fuel from plant sources after asking for, and receiving, his original thoughts.

Where Your Thoughts Originate

I often pose the question, "Where do you suppose your thoughts originate?" Do they originate inside of you, outside of you, or beyond you? What about knowing something versus thinking something? The answer is simply that these are various ways of operating in different states of thinking.

What limits us in our thinking and manifesting is that we mostly operate in the ordinary thinking of our beta brain.

Our brain waves are the measured electrical impulses of our brain while we are in different states of awareness—wakefulness, meditation, sleep, or coma—which are measured in small amounts of electrical charges, or cycles per second.

Our ordinary thinking mind of beta, or our conditioned thinking mind, includes the notions of fear, struggle, us versus them, competition rather than cooperation, and how we are limited and blocked from receiving our good.

What is interesting is that even though we often spend large portions of our time thinking in these ways, that use of our brain occupies more or less only 1 percent of our capacity. When you ask for an original idea, or go to your Source Mind in theta, or seek to expand an idea to a greater capacity than you ever have before, through The One Command, then you begin to live in the other 99 percent of your creative and awesome intelligence.

At the specific moment I asked for an original idea, I was seeking clarification on the question of why and how we get stuck in our limited thinking mind, rather than living and thinking from our Source Mind. I had no idea that the answer was going to show me the origination of our life, from inception to adulthood, but it did.

As with any information, if you find what I have to say valuable, then please embrace it, but if you have a different opinion than I, then embrace that as well. This teaching is about your becoming the gift of who you are, even as I am sharing mine.

Our Human Story

To start, I was shown that we are much more than this physical body and that our greater us is that place in consciousness that we can reconnect to in order to create a greater life.

In fact, as we travel though life, the actual goal is to come into self-love and self-acceptance and to go beyond our stories of who we are and our traumas and drama.

I asked for clarification on how we are more similar as human beings rather than how we are separated by our differences, and I was given a simple explanation.

The story of our beginnings in our human forms was shown to me to start at the moment of the egg and the sperm coming together, instantly creating a unique electromagnetic force field from the DNA of both parents, and the DNA of the ancestors.

It was shown to me that when the body is created, it has an electromagnetic resonance; it has its own tone. That body of the embryo has its own sound and its own personality and physical structure. The soul of who we are, that greater capacity of who we are, comes and resides within this physical body and within the mechanics of this body, and it learns to express itself in this world.

Within our body are the blueprints of our character, dreams, and desires, and in this teaching, you reach into that deepest level of you, even into your DNA, to create lasting wealth: rich and prosperous changes, naturally and easily. We are more than who we are only in this lifetime; we are more than our bodies and this lifetime.

We are here in this world for a great purpose, and that is to learn to love. When we learn to love, we are living in relationship with our state of original Source. We are living in that relationship of who we are in the consciousness that came into our chosen body as an embryo and was born as an infant, that us who lives in our body until we leave the body and continue on in consciousness to play in other universes, and in other forms.

This means that we have great opportunity because there is no limitation to what we can do in our mind; there is no limitation to what we can do in our consciousness.

When we have the awareness of our original Source of who we are before we came into the embryonic state into our physical body, we can realize that we are living through a series of experiences, and we can become more than those experiences, consciously, and we become masters of our destiny.

I don't know how
I am a master of my own destiny.
I only know that I am now, and I am fulfilled!

Chapter Twenty-Four

What We Have in Common

N ext, I was shown how we are related one to another. We are all connected to each other, one to the other. We are all equal in an equality that is simple. This original thought arose within me: what we have in common that connects us—past, race, religion, gender, culture, or physical form—is that we all agreed to be small, defenseless, and powerless.

We all agreed to be born, and to be infants. We all agreed to be affected and programmed by our early childhood; every one of us has had this experience of our humanness. Yet we seem to identify ourselves as uniquely having this experience.

Our experience of the time we were children seems to be our unique suffering, or our unique experience of joy, or our unique experience of limitation, or our unique experience of physical challenge, or whatever is a unique experience to you. Because of this sense of uniqueness, we seem to think that we are separate from everyone else—that we have identified ourselves as the stories of our experience as our identities.

When we forget that our identity is more than those experiences, we become caught in the struggle of living. We become caught in the struggle of "working" our way through life rather than in the pleasure and enjoyment of living. It was shown to me that life is not a lesson, but rather a. . .learning. A lesson connotes judgment, and a pass-or-fail grade, while learning is an ongoing experience. We are here for the learning.

Childhood

We all know that the emotions and experiences of our childhood affect us, but how? When we are children, we have a small body that is our physical form.

In childhood, when an event occurs around us, it is accepted energetically in the body. The experience is processed through the brain, and energetically in the body as a memory. We have many memory chips of experiences that are held within the physical body.

Our subconscious mind is known as the hard drive that stores the feelings from these experiences. When we become the masters of our lives, we are able to say thank you to these memories and to let them go.

We can say, "Thank you. We have practiced longing without satisfaction—enough; we have practiced fear of loss, and lack of love from a parent—enough." We can say, "I have the understanding of this experience, and I am ready for a new reality—one with satisfaction, love, and riches."

Understanding that greater capacity of who you are means releasing your judgments about yourself and others based on your childhood memories, your gender, your religion, your race, your country, your family, and your financial success or lack of success. Release these judgments as an experience, rather than a definition of who you are.

When you refuse to let these memories mature, they consistently repeat the same firing sequence as when you were small, defenseless, and powerless, rather than allowing you to know that time of your life as simply a phase of your life, a portion of your soul experience, and not the truth of who you are. When you let those memories mature and Command another future of good, it must arrive.

A Journey of Change – In Her Own Words

"I am so grateful for what this teaching has done for my life. On the first day of a Commanding Wealth® course, I went into the bathroom and looked into the mirror and said goodbye to my old self because I knew this was going to be a life-changing experience. It was and still is.

My relationship with my husband has changed dramatically for the better. My relationship with my grown children and their families has changed dramatically for the better, especially the relationship with my grandchildren's mother and her husband.

This teaching brought me a life-changing business. This was not the business I was in. I was going in a different direction and I kept running into roadblocks. I was trying to force the situation. After learning how to go into theta and to make The One Command, the doors just opened for a new direction, and my husband and I are taking this direction together. For us to be in such a new position is amazing as well as financially successful in a very short period of time.

I have always been a very insecure person. I always felt like I was not good enough or did not have the education to be successful in my life. I felt that I was not educated enough to talk to professional people such as doctors or lawyers or successful business people. I felt like I did not deserve to be successful. But by practicing The One Command, all that has changed. I speak with ease and comfort, and I know I deserve to be successful.

There is so much going on that it is a continuation of change and growth. I had been out of relationship with my grandkids because of a family dispute, and I wanted desperately to see them. I made The One Command; I don't know how I spend quality time with my grand-daughters. I only know do now, and I am grateful, and I am fulfilled. It wasn't even 24 hours until I got a phone call from their mother; she wanted to know what weekend would be best for us for them to come stay with us. Such a miracle because we hadn't been able to spend time with the girls for over two years!

The stress and difficulty we have had in financing our home ended for us by going to theta and Source and making The One Command; I don't know how greater wealth comes to us. I only know that it does now, and I am grateful and fulfilled.

That day I was on the computer and an ad popped up saying "refinance your home with better interest rates." In my normal thinking brain was the thought that I have bad credit, and as our home was owner financed, no one could help me.

Our credit took a nosedive three years after we bought our home, and we had been turned down to refinance several times in the past. But that gut feeling told me to go ahead and try now. Within 10 minutes, we had a phone call and this man with a thick Irish accent told us what he could do for us, which was unbelievable to us. I mean, he really came through because when they did a title search, the title was in the last owner's dead brother's name. We had trusted the owner when she told us that the title was free and clear. It was a mess! But the angel we met on the Internet a few moments after I made The One Command was able to straighten everything out.

We continued to Command, I don't know how all this works out in our favor with no money coming out of our pockets, only money coming in. I only know it does now, and we are grateful and fulfilled. It took an extra month to make it happen but it did!

It happened! Now we have our home finally financed at a lower interest rate with lower payments. And we are finally getting credit for our mortgage payments, which we were not getting for six years. So our credit scores have now increased as well.

These are just a few of the blessings that have come to us from thinking from another place inside us, the place of possibilities.

Chapter Twenty-Five
Survival Mind

When we made decisions about reality as children, based on what we learned from our families, we made decisions that were in line with the family dynamic in order to survive. You may have had a dysfunctional family—for example, with an alcoholic or abusive parent, or a controlling mother or father, or a rageaholic parent. You may have been raised by someone outside the family, such as foster parents, or you were adopted, or fill-in-the-blank. Even if you were raised by the perfect parents, that might mean having to live up to their expectations of being the perfect child. All the ways in which you coped with your childhood define your thinking about yourself and the world.

We make unconscious choices about how to live our lives as adults, based on the childhood choices we made to be secure, to be safe, to be loved, and to be fed. As children, that is what we are seeking. We are seeking safety and security, and to be loved, and to be fed.

Even when you want to change the way you are living now, you are going to be attracted to those early childhood survival behaviors at the primordial level of your being.

At the tribal instinct level of your brain, you are going to be attracted to the reality you first knew—the reality that you were born into—and when you do so, you are not connecting to your Source

Mind, but rather your survival mind.

For example, a common survival pattern for many adults is to become the helper because as children they survived by "helping" or being "helpful" to the dysfunctional adults who raised them.

Or you may have become the mediator between the warring factions, or you became responsible for your siblings because your parents weren't, and as an adult, you now have an inordinate sense of responsibility to every one but yourself.

Or if there was violence, or anger, or unhappiness, or depression, in your home, you might have had the good sense to hide and disappear until the storm passed. Maybe you would think, "I should go hide and become invisible and play in my make-believe world because my make-believe world will love me no matter what."

The Magical Child

Each and every one of us has created some internal survival strategy in which we are safe. This magical place of safety is where we keep and contain all our real hopes and dreams. This is where the wishful self that wants to be rich resides, the wishful self that wants to make it happen; and at the same time, the wishful self that feels powerless to do so.

For example, if your survival strategy as a child was to disappear and become invisible to be safe, then later on in life when you want an intimate relationship, or want to become rich and prosperous, you will have an inner program determined to keep you invisible, which will fight against your "visible" success.

If you allow yourself to trust, if you allow yourself to be loved, if you allow yourself to be visible and rich, the subconscious program of the little child in you says, "You better not. It is not safe to be seen and to be visible." Your desire for intimacy and success is in conflict with your inner survival program.

The rational adult mind is focused on accomplishing what you want and wonders why there is this seemingly endless struggle for intimacy or prosperity. The reason is simply this: there is a separation between your desire and your ability to have it. This separation between what we desire and our ability to have it is what causes us pain, over and over again.

The way to reprogram those early childhood memories is to Command a change. I don't know how I change my painful beliefs about life based on my childhood. I only know that I do now, and I am fulfilled.

Success Story

One talented man in his late twenties came to a crossroads in his life. He was a successful tile artist with high-paying clients and jobs that included large areas of the town center. He loved his creative work and was well recognized for his talent. But because of the toxic fumes he had inhaled while laying tiles, he had lost a portion of his lung capacity and was seeking to create a new career to improve his health.

When we met, he wanted to open a wood flooring business, but he had always worked for others and was uncertain how to start up his own business. He knew that there was a large ready market for the flooring business. He had found a business space and had product and clients all lined up, but was terrified of going ahead.

We took a look at his early childhood and discovered that his father had been an abusive alcoholic. This young man refused to drink at all. He discovered that his greatest fear for his success was that if he achieved his goals, he would then become like his abusive father.

He Commanded change to release those fears: I don't know how I succeed in my flooring business and retain my kind, gentle self. I only know I do now, and I am fulfilled!

By the simple process of identifying and changing his greatest fear, he changed his inside world, and everything in his outside world changed. He was a financial success within the first month of starting his flooring business, and he had over one million dollars in orders his first year.

Ask for an Original Idea

When you stop living from survival instinct, you begin to function with a new intelligence, an intelligence of discernment with the ability to think and reason, an intelligence that has the capacity to say, "I would like an original idea." And as you add intelligence, you add poetry, you add beauty and the desire for harmony; you add the desire for all that you wish to manifest.

When you think of the capacity of your creative intelligence, think of all that has been designed, manufactured, built, and created in the world. Think of all the philosophers, scientists and inventors; think of all the roads built and dams erected; think of all the skyscrapers, microchips, computers, phones, medical advances, and space travel.

And know this: every idea manifested in the world originated from a thought. Every idea of prosperity and riches originated with a thought. When you ask for an original idea and it arrives, that is your good ready for you.

Chapter Twenty-Six

Creating a New Reality

I n the human consciousness movement, you frequently hear the statement, "You create your reality," just as you are hearing it here.

A reaction to the notion that you create your reality—if your reality doesn't meet your expectations because of ill health, or if you are not well-off financially, or your life is filled with chaos and problems, or you are very rich, yet unhappy—might be that you have done something wrong, that you are suffering because of some past action, or you may ask the question, "Is something wrong with me?"

The notion that you create your reality didn't make life easier for many. In fact, it added an additional burden of guilt and shame. If I don't have the life I desire, and I create my life, what have I done wrong? What did I do to deserve this illness, trauma, financial trouble, or unhappy childhood? Do I have bad "karma," or do I deserve in some way to be punished or to suffer?

To avoid being judged, many acted as if they had a perfect life, while feeling they were living a lie. Our thinking circles in patterns such as If I create my life and my life is not the life I want, then I'm not going to tell people how bad my life is because I don't want them to know what a failure I am. I'm just going to act like it's all working.

This is protective thinking that causes an even a greater sense of separation and unhappiness when we are burdened with the additional thought that If I create my reality and my reality is not good enough, then neither am I, and I must lie about it as well.

The fear of rejection and the fear of others' judgment against us, keeps us silent and separated from what we feel. This is what causes the struggle, this separation of not living in the truth of who we are. When we are able to change our sense of worthiness and speak our truth, we become connected in both our inner desires, and our outer world.

The Truth

The amazing truth of our reality is that we do not deserve to suffer because we have bad karma, or because we are bad people, or because we failed in some way, or because we are paying penance for a past life, or because we are not good enough. The reason we have the reality we have is simply that we have been trained to have it.

We have been trained by the family, individual, or institution that raised us. We have been trained because of the gender of our body, and the expectations of our gender roles; and by the ethnic group, religion, culture, and country in which we were raised; and by the placement of our value or worth in the family.

We have been trained by the amount of freedom or restriction of expression that we have been allowed.

We have been trained by our sense of safety or danger in our environment, and we have made many, many choices about reality based on those experiences. The beliefs that we have accepted become "our reality" and are found within our subconscious mind and are programmed by us into our DNA itself.

**Every emotional thought you have is there
for one thing, and one thing only—that is,
to keep you safe in the world.**

Recognize the power of who you are in your thinking, that your emotional thoughts have either brought your good to you or kept your good from you.

If you are attached to poor, stressful thinking, you do so because it is the only thinking that you trust. You operate from what you have learned, and, as a consequence, you may say truly that you live the Law of Cause and Effect.

What you think affects the results that come back to you. But if the results are less than you hoped for, does that mean you have "bad karma"? In fact, it does not. It means that you were trained to think and feel in such a manner—to not know what having something good, prosperous, loving, and safe would be.

Did you grow up in a poverty-minded, resentful, money-grudging household? Then you believe this is the right way to think to protect yourself. Did you grow up in a rich home where the emphasis was on being rich rather than on being loved? Then you may find it difficult to keep money, or to be rich, because you believe it has to be an either–or choice: money or love.

You Have Been Trained to Think as You Do

Recognize the power of who you are in your thinking. Your emotional thoughts have either brought your financial good to you or kept it from you. You stay attached to poor thinking, or reject rich thinking because that is the only way of thinking that you know.

Did you grow up believing that you had to be secretive about money, or that it wasn't spiritual? Then until you change those notions of reality, you will find it is almost impossible to tell yourself the truth about money, or to believe that you could be spiritual and rich.

Fear, lack, and insecurity are the emotions of your small self. Your small self believes that the fearful experiences from your childhood are true, and that you are powerless to change what you fear.

As an adult, you may find yourself attracted to fearful ideas, which are prevalent almost everywhere. You may experience fears such as, I don't have enough money, the terrorists will get us, the economy is going downhill, I work hard and get nowhere.

Or if you were raised rich, then you may think that money took first place over love and you would be a better person without money, or you may think you have to hide the fact that you are rich to avoid others' scorn of you, a rich person.

Or you may believe that you can never have more than just a little, and if you did, you would be arrogant, sinful, or prideful.

Or when you listen to the television news about terrorists attacking, or the economy's going down the tubes because of x, y, and z, you simply repeat those ideas as true.

You go into agreement with those fears and ideas because, as a child, you were trained to agree with the outside authority of your parents, right or wrong. It's natural to simply go along. It is natural from your tribal, instinctual brain to want to be part of the tribe and to agree with the rest of the pack as well.

We repeat the patterns of our earliest trauma because that is what the subconscious has learned. Now you can learn another way.

In the simple process of going to that greater capacity within you, your Source Mind, you learn to think, feel, and react in another part of your consciousness.

You are in your Source Mind when you lower your brain wave to theta. When you are connected to Source, you can instantly change any and all early traumatic patterns, activate your DNA for wealth, and add knowledge of new experiences that you have never had before.

Learning

Rather than saying life is a lesson, we are here for learning. We are here to go from experience to learning. This is different than saying you are learning a lesson. A lesson means that you are required to learn something, and if you don't, you pass or fail, you are good or bad, you are in the duality of struggle.

If you're not progressing, does that mean you have "bad karma," or does it simply mean that you need more information and a different approach?

Are you stuck?

Are you repeating yourself? And if so, does that mean you are a failed individual?

Or does it mean that you lack confidence in your growth?

When you are learning, it is an ongoing process of experience, amid high moments of the "Aha!"

When you are not experiencing yourself learning, you are thinking in that cycle of the brain that is debilitating, and it is limiting you.

When you are in a moment of "Aha! I understand that learning," then you can say to yourself "I'm done with that old experience. I've drawn that picture. I've made that cacophony of sound in that context, in that ideology, in that emotional band of awareness. I now make a new symphony of music that plays the song. I am loved. I am safe."

Release Past Trauma

One woman shared her experience of being in a bank robbery. She was standing at the teller's window when the bank robber behind her placed his gun on the side of her head, at her temple, as he demanded money. She reports that she went into a complete state of calm and "knew" that she was safe and protected. She went home after the experience unhurt, and that night had a dream of a beautiful nurse carrying her as an infant wrapped in a pink blanket down the hospital hallway with an exquisite feeling of unconditional love and of being nurtured and cared for. She finished her experience of being held hostage with a gun pointed at her head in the moment and in her dream. She completed and integrated the learning.

Others could have had that experience and might have been in therapy the rest of their life from post-traumatic stress, and could again and again recreate the learning in more traumatic incidents.

Go to Source and Command:

**I don't know how I release past trauma.
I only know that I do now, and I am fulfilled.**

SECTION VII
Unwinding

Chapter Twenty-Seven

Point Moment

We make decisions about ourselves emotionally when our brain and emotions coalesce into a certain point: a point in a moment of a decision. That point moment of decision is an abstract. It is not necessarily based on actual events; rather, it is based on the energy of what we decide is true in that moment. This is how we make and retain our thoughts about life, through these point moments when we decide if life is good or bad, safe or dangerous, and whether we can be rich or not. The pain and suffering we go through is from seeking the antidote to those point moments and hoping for it to be different.

The question then is: How many times will you repeat the same experience, one that does not get you what you want? How long does it take for the learning? Once, twice, a thousand times, many lifetimes, repeating the same learning of I know what it feels like to be poor and unhappy, or rich and anxious? Maybe you are ready to say: "I am done and finished with that learning, and declare instead I am committed to live a rich and prosperous, happy and healthy, joyful and spiritual, and sane new life. Maybe I am ready for these learnings?"

Love and Trust

As a child and an adult, you are making decisions about your value, your worthiness, your ability in the world to be who you are, the safety or lack of safety in the world, your ability to give and receive love, and to trust.

The abilities to love and to trust are the two primary emotional bonds we seek. What would that look like, feel like, taste like if you knew what trust of another person was in the cells of your body, so much so that you were comfortable in any situation? What would it feel like to know that you are completely loved?

Imagine that difference as it appeared in your life, when someone said, "I love you," and you were in a loving relationship, and you trusted that. You may not know how to say, "That's wonderful. I am experiencing your love." You may not yet know what it would feel like to trust and love. You might instead say things like, "What's their agenda? What's in it for them? What do they really mean when they say ' I love you'?" It could be just as true that they simply love you. What is in you to love and to accept love?

Another Way to Live

When you reconnect to the deepest part of who you are through your Source Mind, you learn to trust your choices and to trust your own authority once again. You grant yourself permission to live a different, happier, richer, life than your tribe of origin, and by example, lead your tribe forward with you. When you do, magic happens. Your family and society become richer, more harmonious, and more peaceful because of you.

You change whom and what you attract into your life only when you change your subconscious beliefs, as you are doing right now.

Perhaps you have wondered why there are successful people from all economic and emotional conditions who have overcome adversity and the odds to succeed. They have succeeded because they discovered another way to think and feel.

Those who succeed accept ideas and thoughts from the outside world as a choice to believe or not without judgment. They create and manifest from the power within.

Go to Source and Command:

**I don't know how I trust my power within to bring me all my good.
I only know that I do now, and I am fulfilled.**

Chapter Twenty-Eight
The Sacred Self

There is a secret, sacred part of you that you have always protected and kept hidden, no matter what the circumstances of your childhood or the many experiences of your life, that make up the truth of who you are.

If you have been criticized or harmed in any small or large way from the outer world, this part of you is what you return to for safety. In essence you say, "I may have been harmed in such and such a way, but this sacred part of me will not be touched. I will keep this part of me as my secret sacred self."

This is your identity; it is who you are that you maintain, despite what any others have told you or made you believe about yourself.

You may say that even if powerful outside forces have harmed you and affected your life, the truth of who you are is not known to them, and if it cannot be known by others, then you will know it for yourself.

This is your inner self that wishes to express, rather than be repressed by, life. This is the part of you that we invite, here and now, to become that which you are.

The struggles in life, the sense of limitation, the secrets you are supposed to keep, the sacrifices you are asked to make for others, the unrealistic expectations put upon you, or the fear of loss you may have, exist because you are separated from the inner self of who you are and your expression in the outer world. We are continually seeking a remedy for that sense of separation to be replaced with a sense of fulfillment.

It is no longer necessary to suffer when you understand how you think as an emotional being, a tribal being, a human being, and a spiritual being. We can say that in a soul-based sense, you already know much of this material and that you are reawakening to a remembrance of coming back to you, in this place of knowing what you know.

As children, we have innate knowledge within us of the spiritual world of that greater capacity of who we are. The circumstances of our early childhood frame us in the way in which we filter our experience in the future bodies of our adult selves. Circumstances frame us in the genetic encoding of our physical DNA from generations of our ancestors.

Many unknown and unconscious beliefs are brought forward to this moment and point of consciousness, this point of awareness of who we are, in this moment of you as this individual. You knew this before you became a child, and you knew this as a child, and you are ready to know it now again.

It may be said that we forgot to remember and went into the separation of ourselves from this knowledge so that we could have an experience of life. In order to have an experience, we purposefully forgot to remember, until the moment we say, "I do remember" and can live differently now.

Go to Source and Command:

I don't know how I speak my truth from my sacred self.
I only know that I do now, and I am fulfilled.

Chapter Twenty-Nine

Ancestral Memories

nherent in our genetic programming, we carry a tribal instinct for survival that identifies our tribe as a place of safety. We operate on this instinct even if our experience of our tribe of origin, our family, was traumatic and painful. That is why we often attract the same type of friends and partners and experiences: it is safer to be in the reality that we know than it is to live in the unknown.

If it is different, it is dangerous.

When you have this programming of something that you learned that is not something spontaneous within you, and it is something that you were programmed to accept through the people in your environment, your tribe, then it may seem difficult to make a change, even when a change is for the better.

Because we were trained as children to listen and to respond and obey—in order to be fed, to be housed, to be clothed, to be loved—we are trained to listen, to respond, and to obey other people's opinions of us as adults.

When we look outside ourselves for the answers from others (figures of authority, television news, family members, and friends), that is the little child inside of us still seeking permission to be loved and accepted.

Outside Influence

Because we have an innate instinct to want to belong and to be part of the pack, a member of the tribe, the manipulated point of view of the media has a great influence on our psyche in terms of acceptance or rejection. We compare movies, sports events, news on the downturn of the economy, and terrorists on the same bias as the media, and we repeat these ideas as true.

Ask yourself if these beliefs are true: that life is hard, you have to struggle to make it, it is difficult to get what you want, others prevent you from accomplishing your dreams, the economy and world conditions are keeping you from your financial gain.

They are not. The outside influences of the world are simply thoughts that you agree to believe because you fear they might be true. If you are not secure enough in your own thinking and feeling to decide how you want your life to be lived, then you will live your life according to others' ideas of the best or worst life for you. Any conditions of poverty, prejudice, or outside circumstances have only the power that you give to them.

We are conditioned from our childhood to see reality from the point of view of the adult, or adults, who raised us. Because we have been trained to accept the beliefs of our family, or those who raised us, for survival, we have also been trained to accept the influence of others as adults.

Or you may have protected yourself by taking the opposite position: "I am a rebel, and I reject your views." If you still rebel at any new idea or notion, then you gained power as a child by taking the opposite stand that no one will have influence over you, and you thereby limit your good by taking an oppositional stance in general. It becomes difficult to impossible to accept a new notion or idea, even when it is for your highest and best good. Your defense against becomes your prison of limitation within.

As we grow up, we accept influences from those such as teachers, clergy, aunts and uncles, siblings, and the society in which we live. Social pressures and ideas from our peers in school, our neighborhoods, and the poor or rich state of our family also have a significant impact on our beliefs and identity of how we see life and what we think has value. This transfers into our abilities as adults, and creates our reactions and beliefs about social systems, government, corporations, and organizations.

Tribal Mind

To be safe, our tribal mind looks for those who are the most similar to what we know and believe to be true. If you think life is a struggle, then your friends do as well.

Or you may have taken the opposite position and become the isolate, separated from others because you are different and unacceptable, or you may have the thought, "I wouldn't want them to like me anyway because they would try to control me."

Often we seem to find that same abuse, or sense of rejection, or feeling of not being worthy, or stress and worry in every experience and relationship we have.

We seem to attract the same "type" of people and experiences over and over again. We must, because that is what we are attracting to us by our thinking.

Because of our early childhood training to accept what adults tell us, we decrease our ability to know what we believe from within, and we will even attack others if they are in opposition to what we have been trained to think.

Each one of us has kept that sacred part of who we are protected deep within, but the outside influences of our life have trained us to not trust what we know from the intuition and instincts of that self.

We have been trained to distrust what we know because we deny what we know to gain approval from others. Because we desire love and approval from those others, we will protect a position that we think will gain us love and recognition, even at the expense of our own best interests.

The fearful thinking of the collective society, the distrust of others, the fear of terrorism, and the idea of lack and struggle have great power in our thinking for the very same reasons.

We fear that we will not be liked by the tribe if we oppose a popular idea. Taking this to the extreme is the fear that we will be persecuted for those beliefs, or even killed for those beliefs.

Clearing your ancestral programs can open amazing doors of opportunity as you learn to live safely in the world connected to your greater good, your Source Mind. New friends and relationships appear in many mysterious and wonderful ways.

Go to Source and Command:

I don't know how
I clear my ancestral programs of lack and limitation.
I only know that I do now, and I am fulfilled.

Chapter Thirty

Being More than Your Tribe and Family

One of our greatest fears is not that we are limited in our abilities, but rather that we are too much for the world. The two feelings go hand in hand: I am not enough or worthy enough, and I am too much and can harm others by my power.

The unconscious fear that our family will abandon us if we succeed beyond their capacity is inherent in each of us. It is not logical to fear that your father will love you less or reject you if you are more of a success than he is as a man, but you have that fear. It is not logical to feel that your mother will reject you if you are a more successful woman than she is, but this fear often exists deeply within your subconscious.

We know logically that our parents wish a better life for us, but there is this sense of responsibility to them that says, "If I become more than they are, I shame them. If I am happy and healthy and rich, I leave them behind."

There is that within us that says, "If I know how to succeed beyond the expectation of the outside world, and if I can be rich, be wealthy, have an influx of cash, and live an easy, joyful life. . .If I do that, the tribe will reject me, especially if they live a chaotic, stressful life of financial struggle."

One young woman went through this exact journey as she changed her life for the better.

Success Story

A beautiful young woman who desperately wanted to make significant changes in her life began using The One Command on a daily basis.

Her circumstances weren't easy. She had come from a family of alcohol abuse and emotional dysfunction. Her early life was so painful that she died, from an alcohol overdose, for five minutes in the hospital.

When we met, her mother was still actively drinking; even so, they had a close relationship. Her divorced father-in-law also was living with her and her husband. The father-in-law was very critical of how she was living her life, creating a career from her own efforts and skills rather than "getting a job," and told her repeatedly how badly she was doing and that she would fail. In addition, he often spoke badly about her to her husband, which caused friction between them.

She had the desire to create her own business and to teach the world about living from the security and knowledge within ourselves. She looked at her inner beliefs of not accepting her self-worth, and by going to theta, changed those ideas and feelings.

She saw how her family's pattern of chaos was so natural that living differently was something she could only change by connecting to Source and Commanding, I don't know how I succeed in my career and live a happy, rich life. I only know that I do, and I am fulfilled.

She asked for that understanding and continued to trust that she could have the life she desired. She noticed that she was happy and joyful most of the time, even in the face of the harsh circumstances surrounding her.

As she continued Commanding, she noticed breakthroughs within the family. One day her mother called and said, "Honey, we are really worried about you. You have changed so much. You are so different. We don't know who you are. You are happy all the time. I don't understand what is happening to you." After a good laugh, she invited her mom to attend a Commanding Wealth® course we had planned, and her mother attended. Then her father-in law and her husband also attended.

Rather than leave her family behind, they all changed in a greater way than even she could imagine. Her mother returned to school for a nursing career, her father-in law began a new relationship and moved into his own place, and she is well on her way to prosperity in her chosen field. She and her husband own their own home, and have a plan for their future together. Did I mention that she is only twenty-four?

Chapter Thirty-One

Close Your Receptors to Lack

n Candace Pert's book The Molecules of Emotions, she explains that our body/mind brain sends emotional thoughts to receptor sites throughout every cell in our body. Each time we have a thought packed with emotion such as fear of poverty, no money, debt, a sense of being overwhelmed, depression, each time our cells divide and regenerate, more and more receptors are created to harness the feeling of the peptides of those thoughts.

Each time the cells of our body divide and regenerate, receptors increase for the most strongly experienced emotions. We create addictive thinking as our receptors develop a craving for the strongest-felt emotions (mostly our negative ones) and close off to any other emotions or peptides, including those that bring nutrients.

You can redesign and create more and more prosperous receptor sites in the same manner that you have created ones to receive the less useful feelings. The ability to live without fear of financial loss or lack means that you are changing the cells of your body to become addicted to prosperity.

First Response

The emotional programs and thoughts in your unconscious are your ground of being, your baseline of reality, and your first response to thinking, feeling, acting, and reacting.

Changing your concept of reality is an emotional process, not an intellectual one.

It is a spiritual process in that when you travel to the Source Mind first, because you must act in faith (trust without evidence) that your connection to Source disengages your fear-based thinking and attunes you to rich prosperity instead. Only one ingredient is required: the desire to do so.

The process of change from poor thinking to rich, prosperous thinking has to be created with emotions: the emotion of excitement, replacing fear, the emotion of peace replacing chaos and stress, the emotion of joy replacing depression and hopelessness.

Rebuild Your Receptors

If chaos and financial emergencies are normal for you, then your additive thinking resists stability and financial well-being. If sadness, depression, and a feeling of hopelessness, or the thought that others control you or withhold your financial good, is prevalent, then your negative, addictive thinking resists making money easily, receiving cash with joy, and being in control of your own financial good.

When you go to theta by connecting to Source, you can command that your receptor sites be closed to your poor thinking and be rebuilt to receive rich, abundant, easy prosperity as your new way of living.

CONNECT TO SOURCE AND DECLARE:

I don't know how I close my receptor sites to my fearful poverty thoughts.

I only know that I do now, and I am fulfilled.

I don't know how I open new receptor sites to cash, riches, and prosperity.

I only know that I do now, and I am fulfilled.

I don't know how I open to a new level of being money rich and noble.

I only know that I do now, and I am fulfilled.

Success Story

A gentleman in India who owned a manufacturing factory for products sent to the United States called me one day in a dire state of stress. He often feared the worst outcomes in many situations, but this one seemed extremely difficult. He was quite concerned because he had a contract with another company from Norway that had agreed to a partnership. It seemed that the owners were hindering his success and had an agenda that didn't support a true partnership in which they would all benefit. They were not sending the money due his organization, and he was concerned about losing the factory and putting the workers out of work. He had asked for a meeting to solve the problems.

We immediately cleared some of his fearful beliefs with The One Command. I don't know how this partnership succeeds for everyone and we get paid, I only know it does now, and I am fulfilled. As we continued to talk and address his fears with The One Command, he began to have a real sense of peace about the meeting. This was a different state of thinking than he was used to.

He called soon afterwards and said that the meeting was successful beyond what he could imagine: they arrived at new partnership agreements that secured his building and business and greatly benefited both parties. He also received all past-due money at the meeting. He had successfully closed his emotional receptors to the worst-case scenario and almost as if by magic, what he Commanded arrived!

Chapter Thirty-Two

Chemicalization of the Past

S ometimes there is a time delay in reversing the flow of the financial prosperity that you have been sending away from you to a flow toward you. Think for a moment on how long you have emotionally declared your lack through fear and worry.

The time delay is caused by the reorganization and restructuring of your old ways of thinking into new ways of being prosperous. This is a process of chemicalization: burning off the toxic thoughts—making room for the new.

Think about an old-time paddlewheel steamboat traveling down the river in one direction, and then reversing its engines to go in another direction.

The motion of the steamer's paddle reversing its direction is strong and powerful, churning up the water and bringing the debris from the bottom to the top before redirecting its motion forward.

Any time delay in immediately manifesting your new prosperity, health, and emotional good goes through a process similar to the paddle steamer on the river. To reverse direction, the boat has to come to a stop before redirecting its momentum. The time delay is the pause before the new flow arrives. And even with a delay, be prepared for your good to arrive—because it must.

What is wonderful and amazing to know is that no matter what age you are, or no matter what your financial circumstances, this process works every time to change your financial lack to money and prosperity.

The Old Debris

You may expect the churning of the muddy waters to reveal the debris of your old thinking as you redirect yourself to prosperity. Those past thoughts that you had energized with fear will show up as they are on their way out.

Example of Chemicalization

One woman had a beautiful demonstration of The One Command when she declared for new students for her private school, and the next month, three times more students called for enrollment interviews than had ever inquired about the school previously. She was elated. By the beginning of her next term, she had doubled her enrollment.

Some time later, she received notice that an old $7,000 tax bill was due, and she became dejected until she remembered the teaching that anything in the past that is an old debris will show up quite quickly to clear the path for financial gain.

She then realized that it was a blessing to get the bill when she did because, at the time, she had the money to pay it.

Be steadfast in Commanding your prosperity; realize that you have sent limiting thoughts to your future that have to be finalized and brought to a halt.

The residue of those old thoughts has to be churned out of the muddy waters. So keep going forward in faith, with your new way of thinking and being, until you arrive. And then look back at the journey and call yourself proud for what you have done.

Go to Source and Command:

I don't know how
I have faith that my good is on the way.
I only know that I do now, and I am fulfilled.

SECTION VIII
Rewinding

Chapter Thirty-Three

Embrace Change

When we are living in fear, limitation, and lack, we are identified with our small human selves. We have an identity of who we are in our ego structure that is so familiar that we resist changing that identity, even when it causes us pain and suffering. When you choose to become a conscious master of your life, creating what you desire from your Source Mind and applying The One Command, your ego can sometimes become uncertain.

Anyone who experiences a state change from ordinary-thinking beta to the theta state for the first time knows it can be disconcerting. Some people have been programmed to think that the subconscious mind is a place of darkness and is bad, and they feel awkward, and perhaps somewhat fearful, of engaging at deeper levels within themselves.

The exact opposite is true. By going within and attuning to your wonderful subconscious mind, you open the door to greater knowledge, capacity, and understanding. When you go from the subconscious into a higher vibration, you change your attention from your ego, and you dissolve into this lighter self, this spiritual self, and the greater capacity of who you are.

What most often prevents us from making changes in our thinking is the lack of knowledge of what the change will bring. If you have never had the experience of life being easy, and of cash coming instantly to your bank account, and of being rich and prosperous, then the cells of your body, your DNA, and your thinking are not programmed to experience that.

When you change your subconscious thinking, you make changes in your internal space. Your identity shifts, your ego shifts, the cells of your body shift, and you emotionally, mentally, and physically release negative toxic thoughts, feelings, and cellular memories.

We keep fearful and limiting ideas because they bring us the greatest amount of comfort; it is what our subconscious mind knows. The defensive position is to not change; however, our defense then becomes our prison.

When we create a wall of defense to protect us from having another failure, or from someone emotionally hurting us, when we are avoiding men or women because of the pain they caused us in the past, the mind has to remember these painful events to remind us to not have them again. This defense now becomes the prison that we cannot escape. We must stay separated from life, and certain others, to be safe.

You can operate only in a small circle of influence, the one that you have defined as safe. Anything outside that circle is deemed dangerous, or impossible to achieve.

Change Your Beliefs

Consciousness is simple and direct. The easy way to change is to let go of the meaning of your story. The old, difficult way is to think that you must remember to keep yourself from being hurt in that way again. This is not the truth. Remembering becomes the defense that separates you and causes your lack and limitation.

Your brain, body, and the universe are much more forgiving than you are. All that is necessary in consciousness is to redirect a thought. It will create a new reality at that moment. It is that simple.

**This makes the space for your new potential,
and for your dream universe to become the
new foundation of your life.**

What is even more amazing is that when you change a belief, you change it in all directions. Many of us have been driven to help ourselves make life better for our children. When you change a belief, it no longer exists in any direction. By your commitment to help and heal yourself, you heal your ancestors in the past; at the same moment, you heal the future.

Consciousness is similar to writing computer language. It either exists or it doesn't: it is a 1 (on) or a 0 (off). When it is off, it is empty. You can heal your family from alcoholism, poverty consciousness, depression, and all manner of emotional and physical conditions when you heal your thinking. You turn off the programs of that reality, and they no longer exist. If a belief no longer exists in you, you have shifted and changed it everywhere.

The truth is that there is an easy way to live your life. The truth is that when you connect to Source and Command your good, you create from your sacred inner self, and then you have power, you are safe, you are able to love and be loved, and you are connected to your sacred self. The struggle ends.

As you travel into this greater capacity, this extraordinary part of you, the small self may feel its value and importance is being replaced and may not remember who this greater part of you is. The small self asks, "Where am I in the picture? What's going to happen to me?"

You have an identity of who you are in your body and in your ego, an identity in which you are comfortable and familiar. You are learning, in the cells of your body, to make this passage from the ego state of the little self into your greater capacity of your Source Self. As you repeatedly go from your small mind to your Source Mind, you retrain your thinking to know another truth, a grander truth, the real truth about you.

You retrain your brain to create your life consciously—a life of wealth, riches, cash, better relationships, happiness, health, security, and joy that includes your small self. Isn't that a grand joining!

Go to Source and Command:

> **I don't know how I am safe in a new way in the world.**
> **I only know I am, and I am fulfilled.**
> **I am safe when I am connected to Source.**

Success Story

A woman in her fifties had been struggling with painful knees that made her walk stiff legged for over eight years. When she began to Command a change in her life, she wanted more than just financial increase, she wanted an improvement in her physical health and improved relationships in the family. She was having difficulty with her daughter-in-law because they didn't get along at all.

She went through the Six-Step Process up to theta and noticed right away that her knees felt much better. What do you attribute that to, she asked? I replied that going into theta is a natural healing state for our bodies. In addition, you can only have one experience in consciousness: pain off or on, feeling good and healthy off or on, and it seems that her body had moved to the feeling better position on its own. She tested her muscles for the improvement in her knees, and said her strength and mobility was up 35 percent. By the end of three days, she reported that the pain was so diminished that she could bend her knees, something she hadn't been able to do for years.

She called a couple of weeks later to report that not only were her knees still feeling great, in additon, The One Command she had made for a better relationship with her daughter-in-law had come true. The daughter-in-law, who is a physical fitness instructor, was helping her to learn to skip again.

Chapter Thirty-Four

Faith and Trust

I t requires faith to go from your little self in your beta brain to your theta, Source Mind, because you are manifesting something that will appear in your future, yet you have no evidence that it is so. When you realize that the present you have now was created by you, through this process of going from ego to Source and back to physical manifestation unconsciously, then you can see that by using the same technique consciously, you can manifest anything that you desire. It is not questionable to wonder if you will get results in a new way—you must. It is the Law of Cause and Effect in action.

You can come to know the process and procedure of creating your new reality, but you cannot know the results until they appear in your life. You are learning something new, and you are learning it in the cells of your body. You are learning to retrain your brain to consciously create your reality. It requires faith because you cannot know the results beforehand.

By trusting this practice without evidence, you experience a new reality, one that you created. Then you may exclaim in surprise, "I asked, and look, my good is here now." After a few new experiences, your ego may say, "Yes, it is true that I am no longer in charge, but this is a much better way to live, a better game to play. I like it. I am getting everything I ever said I wanted. How can I argue with that?"

As this is a new practice, it is to be expected that new arguments will arise; perhaps even the rebel in you will refuse to give up thinking in old ways. The practice itself gives you the answers to the arguments as they arise, as you continue to go forward.

You have the tools to answer the arguments as they arise, because your arguments are survival programs that are in place for your protection. As soon as you learn that you can be protected in new ways, such as by accepting your good easily, then your little ego self will want to play in this new reality of life.

The parts of you that have protected you in those old ways will join you in new ways once they have the new understanding of safety in each and every new experience. The reasons for your defenses will be replaced with that greater capacity within you to live in peace, safety, trust, and cash-rich wealth. Whether you are rich or struggling financially or in between, we all have our beliefs, and our childhood programming. Every piece of our journey is unraveling the blocks, unraveling the limitations of that programming.

Success Story

One woman from a wealthy family was married with three children and struggling financially. She and her husband made good money, but she could not seem to keep any cash in their bank account. She almost seemed to have a compulsion to give it away. She shared that she was taught as a child to not let others know her family was rich because they wouldn't like or accept her. This was such a strong family belief that she had to pretend another life to her schoolmates and couldn't even bring friends home for fear they would discover she was a "rich girl."

She was also told to give to others to help them and was regularly taken to orphanages and shelters to give food and gifts.

She was taught that others came first and were more important than she was. She said, "I realized that because I was trained to always give, I have devalued any experience of receiving. I have not been able to receive any experience of gratitude or satisfaction for anything I have ever done. I have devalued everything I have to offer and even who I am as well."

She began to Command her good by saying, I don't know how I value my ability and gifts in fair exchange for pay. I only know I do now, and I am fulfilled.

The very next day, she received fifty dollars for her services. She called me and exclaimed that she had earned fifty dollars and had put it in the bank. She explained that this was the first time she had ever felt her value—when she received fifty dollars for her work and kept it for herself.

That was her transformative experience.

She didn't give it away.

She kept it and felt that she was valued and rich.

Go to Source and Command in theta:

I don't know how
I trust that I change my life with The One Command,
I only know that I do now, and I am fulfilled.

Chapter Thirty-Five

Only Now

I t helps to change your fixed, subconscious programs when you realize that there is no such thing as "a past." There is only you now, experiencing thoughts and feelings now.

Right now, in the now, you are recreating a thought that you have had many times. You may call it a memory, but you are thinking it now, and recreating sorrow, pain, and grief, or happiness, security, and joy—now.

You have every right to change, rearrange, and improve your thoughts about your life—right now.

The past is not sacrosanct. It happened, and there is nothing that you can do about it. Yes, that experience did happen, yet there is much you can do to change the decisions you made about you and the world as a result of that experience.

A belief from your childhood is something that you created in a moment, with the best evidence you had at the time, in order to survive and to receive love.

Does it serve you now to believe that life is dangerous, or you can't trust the other guy, or you have to watch out so others won't hurt you, or that you have to work hard to earn a living, or that you have to suffer to learn and grow, or that others can succeed but not you, or that you have to accept your lot in life?

If it no longer serves you, then keep your memories, but change your decisions about you and about life.

What would that be like?

What if it were just as true. . .that you can trust the other guy, that others want to help you, that it is easy to earn a living, that it is preferable to learn and grow even more in ease than in suffering, that you and others can succeed, and that you can create any life you desire?

When we are deeply identified with our beliefs, there is an even greater fear that if we change our suppositions about the nature of reality, we will be too vulnerable to defend ourselves against danger. The more traumatic a childhood we had, the more deeply engrained are the beliefs about the lack of safety in the world, and from others.

You are being shown how to replace that emptiness with a new understanding, one that is the truth of what you desire: to be safe, loved, prosperous, creative, spiritual, kind, joyful, and happy in your life.

It is possible to replace those old beliefs with these new ones, because these experiences that you truly desire, exist somewhere in consciousness.

If any one person knows how to be rich and happy, or how to be wealthy with kindness, spirituality, and ease, or how to speak his or her truth and be safe, then everyone can have that same experience.

What you discover when you lower your brain waves to the theta brain frequency, and connect to Source, and communicate directly, consciousness to consciousness, is that you can accept a "direct link" of what it does feel like for life to be easy as you increase your wealth, happiness, and prosperity.

Once the cells of your body, mind, and emotions receive this new information, then the old programs have fulfilled their function. They have kept you safe up to this point in your in life, and now you can be safe in another way. They can let go and rearrange into a new belief, a new way of living.

Success Story

No matter what our age or circumstance, it is possible to redirect lack and limitation into prosperity and success in new and extraordinary ways as exemplified by this wonderful sixty-four-year-old woman on disability who began to Command a new financial future for herself. She had been very active with many friends and business contacts until devastating spinal damage changed her life. She was struggling with depression and the small amount of money her disability provided until she began to Command for her health, emotional well-being, and great increase in her finances.

One major obstruction to changing her circumstances was a long-held idea that what she had to say was of no value. Why would anyone want to listen to me, she often thought. This is where she began to apply The One Command first. I don't know how what I have to say has value. I only know that it does now, and I am fulfilled. She went up into theta and made her Command and saw all the old ideas of her "non-value" unwind and disappear out of her DNA, and she saw instead people listening to her with a positive response.

Things began to improve immediately. She noticed how satisfied she felt when sharing her ideas with others and how well they responded. During this time, she met a businessman who was looking for someone to promote his product, a wonderful energy light machine that improved health rather quickly.

She thought, "Well, why not me?" and began to promote the product. The results were beyond imagining. Every person with whom she promoted the product responded favorably, and within three weeks she had earned over $4,000 in commissions. Within six weeks, she had changed her financial flow to such an extent that she got two machines worth $16,000 for herself and is now still making great commissions. Her only remaining problem was notifying disability that she no longer needed their funding.

Take a moment:

Ground, Align, Go to theta, Command, Expand, and Receive.

I don't know how I change my limiting beliefs about myself and replace them with a new understanding of peace and satisfaction. I only know that I do now, and I am fulfilled.

Chapter Thirty-Six

Clearing the Playing Field

T o clear the playing field in your favor, you want to look at what ideas don't support your dreams, and then clear them. How were you trained by the outside world not to support your desires? How were you trained to feel inadequate? How were you trained to feel that others aren't inviting you into their lives, aren't on your team, wouldn't want to help you, and wouldn't want your product even when it is worthwhile and valuable?

What in you has been trained to think that way? What in you has been trained to say that people aren't safe, people want to be left alone, or that you might be rejected if you tell them your ideas? Those are limiting beliefs that are not the truth.

These are simply ideas and emotions that we have been programmed to accept. We have been programmed to accept these ideas in order to be accepted, approved of, and loved.

We have been told to sacrifice even the possibility of our dream for approval, rather than to dare to be unique, magnificent, and wonderfully who we are. We have been told there is a certain behavior model we must follow to be successful, such as don't make waves or don't rock the boat. You can fill in the blanks with the thousands of beliefs about how we have been trained that limit our good.

When you are operating in the greater capacity of you, and you are operating from love, and the desire of right action, and you are operating from that greatest part of you, with integrity, with honesty, with a desire to be of service in the world, to play in the world, and to be rich in the world, and to have the world be a right world, then you are in that stream of reality that you are creating and bringing to others.

You are offering that good to anyone with whom you are inter-acting, at the same time you are offering the opportunity to buy a beautiful product—something good for the body, a product that heals or an idea that changes lives.

Unwinding negative beliefs and ideas of limitation, and rewinding new prosperous ones into your DNA and your mind and emotions, is the key to financial success. The key to success in achieving your desires and maintaining your dreams and your goals is knowing that there is an unlimited supply of financial good at your fingertips.

You may ask, "Why do others have great financial success, and why don't I?"

What is the difference? What would prevent you from being as rich as the person next to you?

The only thing required is the desire to do so.

When you have the desire to be rich and financially well-off, then you are focusing on an idea.

When you get an idea of how to do it, then you take that idea forward by your action steps.

By going to Source and turning on the theta brain wave and connecting to that deeper part of you and Commanding, I don't know how, and turning it over to that greater capacity—a more creative, spontaneous, natural part of you, the untrained part of yourself—you succeed.

You succeed by living in the part of you that has an unlimited potential of ideas, that has the idea that it might be just as true, that the world is an easy place in which to live, and by thinking, What if it were just as true that it is natural and ordinary to be richer and richer and more joyful?

What if it were just as true that you are able to accomplish that idea? You are creating reality in the direction in which you are focusing.

If you move your consciousness into another realm, into a realm of masters creating reality, then you begin by focusing on:

I don't know how to create a new reality for myself.
I only know that I do now, and I am fulfilled.

Focus on this: I have the desire to create that reality for myself, and that is all that is required to change reality—to have the desire and to stay steadfast in my desire.

When you practice operating from within yourself, from the power of who you are in your capacity to create any success for yourself, then the world responds.

Reality responds. Reality resonates with your desire, because your desire becomes the strongest desire to be fulfilled. Your desire becomes the tickle in consciousness with the other person or people you are playing and interacting with, because you are making an invitation to a new reality.

Dialogue

Asara: Let's investigate what can be cleared. What in you would you like to change?

Guest: For me, it is a "lack" consciousness and buying into what has been.

Asara: Do you have anything specific?

Guest: I want to find out what I really want.

Asara: In what sense of having what you really want?

Guest: Trouble is, I know it is me.

Asara: Let's just clear it by investigating it. We can clear what the limiting belief is just by investigating it. What prevents you from having what you really want?

Guest: I don't feel supported in that, I guess.

Asara: You are not supported in having what you really want. When you are not supported in having what you really want, what does that look like to you? Who is not supporting you?

Guest: Other people, the universe ...

Asara: When they are not supporting you in having what you want, is there a reason why they don't want to support you?

Guest: I guess it comes back to, I am afraid they don't want what I have to offer.

Asara: Okay, so what you have to offer is not valuable. Then you would have to say, "I am not valuable." So I am not valuable. Okay, so let's just do The One Command. Just go ahead and say: I don't know how I am valuable.

Guest: I don't know how I am valuable now. I only know I am, and I am fulfilled.

Asara: Now close your eyes, ground, align your heart, go to theta, and Command mentally, I don't know how I am valuable and supported in the world now. I only know I am, and I am fulfilled. Expand that into an idea greater than you, receive that knowledge, that good, and when you are ready, come back into your body, unwind the old programs in the cells of your body and DNA, and rewind your DNA with gratitude. Thank you.

She takes a moment.

Asara: Did you experience anything physical when you went up to theta and made your Command?

Guest: Yeah, when I said it, I had an exhale release. I feel great. I feel different and empowered.

Asara: Great. Thank you.

Chapter Thirty-Seven

Shift Out of the Old

By the simple process of The One Command, you are shifting out of the old and into the unlimited potentiality of any probable future.

When you identify what limits you by telling the truth, by saying what it is that you believe opposes you and shift that with The One Command, you are un-creating an old idea. A belief is just that, an idea that you take with you in your mind. When your mind can release that idea, then you come back into random possibilities.

For example, you might ask, "Is there a God out there who is telling me I can't have what I want? What is opposing my having what I want?" If you have the emotion of being opposed, it is an idea that you have been trained to accept, and you continue to view life through that lens.

What if it were just as true that there is no opposition? We are just making opposition up. Opposition is something we imagine emotionally because we were powerless as children. We are now moving into our ability to be in our power, and it is unfamiliar to be in our power. I don't know how I am in my power now, and I am fulfilled. I only know that I am.

You answer every fear by stating The One Command. It is a physical event. When you state The One Command, it is neurologically de-linking the old, fearful ideas. It is putting you back into the potential.

When you say, I know that it is so now, and I am fulfilled, you are sending that into the world. The world is now hearing that declaration—the world supports me, and I support the world. I am supported, and I know what it feels like to be supported in the world.

I know the "is-ness" of support in the world; I know that the world is a supportive place to live. I know what it feels like to support others with my gifts of what I have to bring to the world, and I know how to be well received. I am well received with my gifts in the world, and I receive gifts well.

Vision Boards and Support

Now, in addition to reprogramming the inner self, you can add images of your dream on a vision board to view every day. When you shift on the inner world, and have the reminders in the outer world, you have 100 percent availability of success—100 percent availability of achieving your goals.

It must occur. It has to occur because you are now creating 100 percent of your reality with your thinking. When you change your thinking through all the levels of your being, through the DNA, through the neuro-net connections in your brain, through your emotional body, through your vision and ideas, through the sounds that you accept and listen to, when you change at all those levels, you change your reality: the new reality must arrive.

Don't even worry about it. It has to happen. You go from success to success to success. Even as you succeed, the old ideas of not accomplishing your goals will come up, as they must; this is a process of change.

When those ideas come up, you go back to The One Command, take time to connect to Source through the Six Steps, and then

Command: I don't know how I continue to achieve my success, and I am fulfilled. I continue to achieve my success financially, and I am fulfilled. I continue to achieve my financial goals, and I am fulfilled; I only know I do now, and I am fulfilled!

You continue to go forward with your growth. As you practice this, you are including faith; that is, you are experiencing trust without evidence. You are operating in faith of a new reality's arriving, without evidence of it arriving, until it does. Then when it arrives, you have evidence. And you did that.

Then when the next success arrives, you have more evidence, and then your subconscious mind begins to get that tickle inside again. Hey, this is great. It's working. Whatever this is, it's working. I like it. Then you get more and more ingrained in being a master of reality, in defining your life according to your own desire. And you are making that connection to that greater capacity within you.

You are designing your life either by accident or design. Why not become the architect of your own success?

Success Story

A young gentleman with a wife and a baby had moved to a new town, because he was looking for a better opportunity. The moving expenses left them very short of cash. Immediately, the young man went out looking for regular work, but he was repeatedly turned down.

Their financial situation got so dire that they were given an eviction notice and had only one week before they would be removed from their flat.

The young man even applied for public assistance to keep a roof over their heads, but was turned down because he owned some "property"—an old Volkswagen bus.

He had just recently heard about the principles in Commanding Wealth®, and was willing to try anything. He began to Command, "I don't know how I pay my rent to stay in my flat and keep a roof over my family. I only know that I do now, and I am fulfilled." And he imagined that cash arriving on his doorstep.

He practiced this daily while still looking for work.

The day before he was due to be evicted, there was a knock on his front door and he went to answer it. The fellow at the door said that he noticed the Volkswagen bus in the yard and wanted to know if he would sell it for a thousand dollars, the exact amount owed for the young man's back rent.

The fellow said he had the cash on him if he was willing to sell. The young man accepted the cash for his car and gladly paid his rent.

His miracle had arrived right in time and on his doorstep.

He also was hired for work the very next day.

SECTION IX
The Attitude of Wealth

Not only are you bringing something great into the world,
you are teaching the world, by your greatness, how to be great.

-Asara Lovejoy

Chapter Thirty-Eight

Commanding Wealth® as a Way of Living

The inconceivable yet simple truth is that there is an easy way to live differently. The truth is that when you connect to Source and create from your greater capacity, you have great power, you are safe, you are able to love and be loved, and you are connected to your own importance and the importance of others. The struggle ends.

The Commanding Wealth® way of living is to live consciously connected to Source, to that greater capacity of who you are. The better way is to learn to trust and have faith without evidence, and to become the master of your own destiny.

This is a shift in your identity that is the mastery state of mind. This new way to create your life is to focus on what you wish to create, and to de-concentrate on that which you no longer wish to create.

When you seek the truth of who you are and you neurologically retrain your brain to operate in theta, you find yourself speaking the truth of who you are from your Source state, naturally, without having to cover up your identity; your life begins to work in more and more wonderful and mysterious ways.

The more you live connected to Source, the more you live in

freedom, the more you live in prosperity, the more you receive the good that is yours.

You have an incredible brain. You have an incredible emotional body. You have an incredible intelligence, and when you tap in to your own intelligence and learn to link to Source at will, then you create your life without fear, and by conscious, rather than unconscious, choices.

When you go into the theta brain wave and link to Source, you literally become unattached to the story of your life; you become "non-attached"; you become the observer.

That doesn't mean that you aren't passionately involved. You are passionately involved and non-attached to the story. You have more distance to observe and to look at the choices you are making.

When you develop your ability to operate in your theta brain wave, you are creating new neurological brain patterns—new pathways of thinking, receiving, creating, and expressing.

Neurologically, you are physically de-linking the old ways. You are physically changing reality within the cells of your body and your DNA.

Now you can be restored to that ability to make new, undiscovered conclusions about life—ones that are safe, rich, prosperous, healthy, and yours to enjoy.

What would that be like? Here are some qualities of living a rich, prosperous, and emotionally satisfying healthy life:

You make good choices.
Your friendships act as ballasts.
You increase your bank accounts.
You establish good relationships.

I live in a state of immeasurable wealth and abundance. I live in a joyful, loving, rich universe. I know the truths of the universe in my rich life with money, loved ones, and friends, and in the world. With my Command it is done, and it is so! I'm so wealthy I don't know how much I have. I have as much as I want to spend, and I always have more than I need. I spend what I want, buy what I like, live a rich life, and give large sums of money back to the community to help others. I think big. I provide jobs. I share when and where I can. I take what I earn, either through a job or self-employment, and pay as I go. I expand gradually and realistically, and I invest a portion of what I earn to build a financial future. I have good, reliable savings, and I enjoy my everyday life to the max with loved ones, family, kids, and friends. I make appropriate charitable contributions and tithe regularly.

Chapter Thirty-Nine

Receiving

You have the ability within your mind to be in a different portion of your brain, the portion of your brain that isn't programmed yet. It doesn't have a pattern yet. You can program that portion of your brain to be the master that you desire to be, because that portion of your brain is not programmed with the collective unconscious or negative thinking. It is that greater capacity of unlimited thinking, or thinking in unlimited ways.

The path to bring your good to you is by expanding your consciousness into a cauldron of receptivity for your greater prosperity.

You have the ability to receive the good that comes to you, energetically and emotionally.

As you expand and increase your capacity for that emotional good, your financial good follows.

The path of mastery is first to be in charge of your thinking, not with the old effort, or the old way, or by struggle, but by accessing the deeper brain waves within you in the theta state. In that theta state, when you say "I don't know how," you stop your old negative thinking. I only know that I create this good in my life now, and I am fulfilled. You thrust it into the universe and receive with gratitude.

I don't know how must be used to stop the negative thinking because negative thinking will always arise with your desire. The minute that you have a desire, it will be matched by your old thinking that says, "No, you can't have that desire," until you train yourself to a new experience.

You stop the old thinking and go forward with I don't know how. I only know I have it now. That is the second step.

In the second step, you see the flow of your good coming to you. You are seeing and imagining all that good coming to you. You are seeing and imagining all of the cash that you want coming to you in the cash consciousness of playing with money and prosperity and emotional well-being and health and happiness and physical agility and all of the qualities that you want. You are seeing them coming to you.

What Can You Imagine That You Can Have

The first step in receiving your good is to Command that it is so. I don't know how I receive my financial and prosperous good. I only know that I do now, and I am fulfilled.

This process is so simple: whatever you don't have or don't know, you can simply Command to arrive and it must. It is the law!

Next, play with the idea of what you are able to have in your life.

Look at what being rich means to you other than the idea, I want to be rich to solve my financial problems.

You say, "I want to be a rich person because that would mean freedom to me." But emotionally, how would your life change? Emotionally, would you really be a different person once you are rich, once you have a great financial flow?

Quite frequently, what happens is beyond your expectations of financial accomplishment. It is so wonderful. It is so much more than you anticipated having. The ego structure that is not used to this idea must be prepared for receiving your good. It may experience a loss of identity because your old identity is tied up with the struggle. Your identity has been on the journey of struggle, not in experiencing the accomplishment.

To go forward and expand in all ways, you must make yourself a viable receptacle for receiving this good.

You want to know the emotions of your success and of receiving your financial good so that you may have it. I don't know how I receive my financial and prosperous good. I only know that I do now, and I am fulfilled.

Imagine More

Imagine that right now you have all the financial good that you have ever imagined you wanted. Just imagine that you have all that financial good now. You have so much cash that you have it just stacked up in your bank account. You have so much cash that you don't worry about writing a check. You don't even have to think about it. If you want something, the cash is there for you in great measure. To pay a bill is so easy. You are accomplishing your prosperity with your environment. You have the kind of home you want, or the kind of car you want. You have the ability to provide for the people you love and to give gifts of cash.

Who are you in that? See how you are. Who are you? What do you look like? What is different? What do the cells of your body feel like? Emotionally, what do you want now? What is next in your life? The struggle is gone.

You have already done it. It is accomplished. What is your life's purpose once you have already accomplished that good? Once you have attained your financial goals? What is your life's purpose? Just notice what you are noticing. What did you notice?

Some Stories of What Others Have Noticed

First Guest: To me, it is helping others—teaching them and showing them and coaching them to do it.

Asara: Great. So your life purpose is in a greater idea and greater capacity than the simple fulfillment of your financial goals.

Second Guest: Thank you for that. The feelings were wonderful. What I saw was that I was doing what I was already doing. I was just doing it without the struggle. It was really nice. What I saw was the degree to which I contributed to others' life increase, and I could do it in a lot less stressful way when I didn't take the struggle with me into that.

Third Guest: A good feeling, of course. Relief that all that stress was gone. I was in that seeking state of "now what?"

Asara: So you are still looking; you don't have an answer yet. That's a beginning.

Fourth Guest: For me, the freedom just felt like breaking out of chains. I was just feeling how constricted I have been and the lack of that freedom. It was coming unshackled.

Chapter Forty

Increase Your Capacity

When you have an idea that is greater than you, you are creating a vacuum from that space around you of your own ego identity. You increase your capacity to receive your rich, abundant good.

This is a natural, easy way to grow.

This is a natural, easy way to blossom and to flourish and to expand and to increase your capacity.

Imagine the cells of your body expanding and increasing in prosperity as they receive more and more emotions of success.

You have been addicted to those feelings of struggle. You have been addicted to fearful thoughts. You have been trained to have them from the family that raised you, from their neurology, from their belief structure.

You have modeled the environment around you at your tribal, instinctual level for survival. Your biology and the cells of your body are trained to identify and resonate with what is in your environment, and to unconsciously seek something similar for your safety.

In a lot of ways, you stopped maturing, stopped evolving; you stopped yourself from waking up to how your life could be different.

Rather than attempting to overcome the struggle, resonate with something different, by Commanding your good.

When you resonate with something different,
in a greater way, in a greater capacity, it is simply effortless.

Imagine one of those television ads for laundry detergent in which the detergent weaves its way through the clothes, disengaging the dirt, which lifts up and floats away. Have you seen those ads? You see the detergent molecules go in and lift the stain off the clothes, and the dirt simply floats away. You ask, where did the dirt go? It just lifts up and dissolves. When you do it the easy way, you simply go into that greater capacity of you, and your old beliefs dissolve.

Accept a Greater Good

When you go into that greater capacity of you, you are accepting something unfamiliar and unknown.

You can't know it yet because you have never had it, but you are going after it.

You go to Source and Command, I don't know how I have that good in my life where I am satisfied and peaceful every day in my activities on my way to my prosperity. I only know I am now, and I am fulfilled.

When you are in that resonance field, you begin to focus on that greater good, that satisfaction, that peaceful state, that trust in the universe that says, I am prosperous now, and I have the tools now. I know how to do this.

"I am a master, and I am simply changing the focus of what I am manifesting. I am not focusing on the fear of what I may not have. I am focusing on how and why and what I want in my life. That becomes my new adventure. It becomes my new adventure to create and manifest and to discover, to stay in the excitement of the new discovery of what I wish to create for myself."

This is beyond what I know right now.

You say, "I don't know what that greater good is for me.
I only know there is a part of me that knows that greater good,
and it is mine now, and I am fulfilled."

When you practice allowing yourself
to be in the not knowing,
miracles arrive in your life.

You Start with Your Desire

You start with you desire, but you don't know how to do it. You Command your financial prosperity and your good to magnetize it to you, then you receive inspiration and ideas, and then you actualize the idea with your action steps in the world.

The miracle is the inspiration and all the ways your good arrives beyond your ability to know it in advance.

And then somebody comes and knocks on your door to help you release an old program or calls you to say I want your product or your services because you are making a concentration on the greater good.

You become the master accomplishing it, and all of a sudden your ego says, "You know, I really don't know how that happened."

You absolutely don't know because you cannot know with your cognitive, small mind.

You cannot know it.

It is so much greater than your beta mind and is in such a subtle form of your intelligence that you cannot know it through your conscious mind.

You can know it as the result of the activity of your thinking of what you choose to magnetize to you, and you can know it as expectancy about when it is going to show up.

This Becomes Your New Reality

You are now operating in this new reality of your good arriving, and you prepare yourself for receiving it by directly experiencing what it feels like to be in that satisfied state of success now, rather than saying, I can't be in that satisfied state of success until I have achieved my goals.

You begin to say, I live this now. I live this state of prosperity now. I live this mastery now. I am in this state now. That's who I am, right now, today.

Then you Command the experience of knowing what it feels like to be peaceful about money and your mastery.

Go to Source and Command:

**I don't know how I live my prosperous mastery.
I only know that I do now, and I am fulfilled!**

Chapter Forty-One

Know Your Financial Good Before It Arrives

You Command your wealth and prosperity right now, and that becomes your new operating system. It becomes your new hard drive. It becomes the new wiring for your subconscious mind.

You become attracted to your rich way of thinking. When you become attracted to that as a new way of thinking, energetically, the world matches you, and you increase the evidence of that prosperity, and you receive more and more evidence. The evidential procedure then empowers you again and again.

All of this is instantaneous in the experience inside of you, but it is cumulative in terms of your impact in the world, and the world's impact back to you. That is cumulative because you are lifting out and away from that smaller reality and moving into greater levels of consciousness.

As you do so, you are not only changing your consciousness, you are also changing the world's consciousness because of your quantum effect in the world. You are making a difference in the world—a great difference in the world as you make a great difference in your own thinking.

When you are reprogramming yourself for this understanding of new qualities as a daily activity, you are rerouting the old, addictive thinking patterns to a new pattern. It has more power than addiction. It just is.

It becomes an "*is-ness*" within you.
Play with these new conditions of knowing, and
receive the knowledge of the emotions: *I don't know how.*

I only know I am secure in my everyday activities. I only know I am rich inside of me financially. I only know I am peaceful about money. I only know I am successful in accomplishing great things, and I feel safe in the world,

I only know that I am now, and I am fulfilled.

Make room in yourself for this feeling of safety as you become more present in the world, and notice people recognize you—that you have a greater relationship with more people—and know that you are safe.

I don't know how.

I only know what it is in me to be strong and prosperous.

I only know what it is in me to be rich, really rich, and to have lots of money, to be in that financial state of richness where I am at ease over my money.

I only know what it is in me to have and endless supply of money.

I only know what it is in me to be rich and to be welcomed within the world.

I only know what it is in me to have an idea, act on it, and have it work out.

I only know what it is in me to implement my ideas and have them accepted.

I only know what it is in me to have life be easy.

I only know what it is in me to be joyful in my life, to be joyful, rich, and successful in my life.

I only know that it is in me now, and I am fulfilled.

Make It Real

This is real. I want you to know this is real. What you are experiencing here and what you are discovering here is real. What you are experiencing is creating your life.

What you discover is how easy it is to change the magnetic attraction around you through the emotions of your thinking and The One Command.

You don't have to know the story. You don't have to unwind the story of how or why you are who you are. You can do that if you want to and that is okay, but energetically you can create that vacuum, like the spot disappearing in the laundry, by being, thinking, and feeling in a greater capacity.

As that energy comes in, it is like an invisible ultrasound resonance of cash, and prosperity going into your DNA at the subatomic, cellular level and jiggling the cells of your body into a new reality, tickling it into a new idea.

Releasing old thought forms and old ideas of limitation.

They dissolve as you go to Source and create a vacuum as you dissolve the old boundaries of your thinking to that greater capacity of your unlimited self.

As you go to Source and create a vacuum, you dissolve the old boundaries of your thinking and expand into that greater capacity of your unlimited self.

When you pull your thinking from the universe in a greater under-standing, you return to that spontaneous experience of life as a child. You return to that spontaneous sense of adventure of not knowing the answers and of exploring the possibilities.

Go to Source and Command:

I don't know how I explore the possibilities.
I only know that I do now, and I am fulfilled.

Chapter Forty-Two

Prepare for Your Wealth

In truth, we have no idea how the world works. We have knowledge and rules about science and gravity and thoughts and reality, but it is our understanding only. It is the understanding of our small, limited self.

I say, respectfully and joyfully, bless all those parts of you that want to continue to grow: that is your greater self who wants to have new adventures. That is the part of you who wants to go to that greater place within you, to have more expression inside of you, to accomplish greater good inside of you, and to feel at peace and ease about it while you are doing it, and to be prepared for it to be good.

Prepare a grand cauldron large enough to receive all your plenty, a cauldron as deep as the greatest depth at the bottom of the ocean that receives and contains cash, jewels, gold, and an infinite supply of your good. Know that you have that in your bank account, in your cash flow, and in every transaction for your prosperity and wealth.

Prepare yourself to have it be easy, joyful, and with bountiful delights.

Prepare yourself emotionally for your successful financial destiny.

The most difficult portion of manifesting your good is in receiving it. Did you know that gamblers, for example, get depressed when they win big? The struggle is the addiction. And I think many of us have heard the high number of bankruptcies that happen with lottery winners. They were not prepared for their good.

Rather than focusing on recycling the ideas in your small brain and telling yourself how you are not having those things, you want to focus on having what you want coming to you, and then you want to be prepared to receive your good in a great way. You want to be prepared for being rich. You want to be prepared for being healthy and be prepared for being loved.

The most common failure of people on the success path is not in their ability to manifest or create; it is their inability to maintain and to receive the good that they have created.

You are teaching yourself the mastery of how to receive that good in your life, in the cells of your body, in your DNA, in your brain, and in all of the ways you wish to express your wealth in joy and happiness. You are teaching yourself to live differently, naturally, and easily.

Dialogue

Guest: I really relate to not being prepared for it to be good. It felt like a jolt to realize I've only been prepared for it to be bad. That needs to change. There was a real Aha! I would like to change that, to really anchor that in, to be prepared for it to be good.

Asara: Okay! Where in your childhood do you think you learned that? Who taught you to be prepared for it to be bad?

Guest: Mom always told me to be prepared for the worst. Bless her heart. She is good at it. Her being prepared for the worst has helped us out on several occasions, but it has become an unconscious habit. It is not where I want to be. I want to be in a prepared state for the good.

Asara:
Let's change the belief that being prepared for the worst is necessary to be safe. Ground, align, go to theta, Command, I don't know how I am prepared for it to be good. I only know that I am now, and I am fulfilled; expand that idea, and receive in gratitude.

Guest:
(After the process.) Oh, thank you. Yes. That is delicious.

New Guest:
I have a comment that I want to share. When I was getting ready to move forward in my practice, Asara and I were talking, and I kept saying, "In the worst-case scenario I can. . ." Asara would stop me immediately, and I noticed that when I thought about what the worst and the least I could get by with, the smallest amount I could expect, my body would constrict. I could feel my stomach just tightening and my energy field would start collapsing. When I made The One Command, I don't know how to prepare for the best. I only know I do now. I don't know how to prepare for all the good that wants to come to me. I only know I am now, and I am satisfied. That reversed it and I still am safe, and I get directed to things that need my attention and more good comes to me. I just wanted to give a little testimony that when you are thinking about that worst-case scenario, that is what you get.

Chapter Forty-Three

Forgive Yourself

Out beyond the ideas of

Right doing and wrong doing

There is a field

I'll meet you there

-Rumi

Your emotional thinking, not outside circumstances, is responsible for either your state of lack or your financial good. You are truly the creator of your world. If you blame yourself or make judgments against yourself because you aren't having the experience of wealth you desire yet, then let go and forgive the mistakes of your thinking.

After all, most of it has been programmed into you, and now you have an opportunity to choose your own programs of health and wealth.

Example of Change

One woman I know got trapped in her efforts to get child support. Yes, the child support was due and it was important that the father provided it, but she saw it as necessary for her survival. She woke up one day, and the kids were gone, and she had no means to provide for herself. She saw someone else as the source of her financial good, rather than Source and her intelligence!

She was bitter at the position she found herself in and was mostly angry with herself. She began to Command her forgiveness, I don't know how I forgive my financial mistakes. I only know that I do now, and I am fulfilled.

As she Commanded forgiveness for herself, a peaceful calm began to prevail in her thoughts. That in itself was rewarding, but she also noticed that she was enjoying herself. Her friends were coming around more frequently too because of her improved attitude. One friend she hadn't seen for quite a while told her that their company had just lost their bookkeeper and they were stressed about getting a replacement. The woman had bookkeeping experience and was hired for the job. Once she had Commanded self-forgiveness, her world of opportunity arrived.

Forgive yourself, forgive others who have taken money from you, forgive debts against you, and bless those who have loaned money to you.

Be grateful to the utility and phone companies because of the faith they gave to you—that you will pay for the services they provide in advance of payment.

If you have a difficult time with the concept of forgiveness, or any other new concept, ask yourself one question: Is it worth it to open to the new possibility that there is another way to think, to get results, and to be safe?

You know the results that you have now from your thinking. Wouldn't it be amazing if the new way gave you the results that you have always wanted?

Money resentments and money grudges must be thought of as past history, a history that you have left behind.

One young man told us of the experience he had during the break of a Commanding Wealth® seminar.

I went to the park with my family for lunch, and I looked up and saw a friend who owed me money. Rather than feeling resentment, since I had not seen him in over a year, I went over to him and said hello.

After our greeting, he looked at me and said, "By the way, don't I owe you some money?

I said, "Oh, yeah, but don't worry about it," and he said, "No, I can pay you now, and I want to pay you. What is it I owe you, about a hundred dollars?"

"Yes," I replied.

He immediately left the park and returned in fifteen minutes with the cash in hand from the ATM.

I would have missed this opportunity in the past because I would have been stuck in a place of judgment and anger, and I would have left without speaking to him.

Forgive your old way of thinking, and watch the circumstances of your money and finances change for your good

Begin Where You Are

Take time to go through the Six Steps: ground, align, go to theta, Command, expand, and receive in gratitude—and begin where you are.

I don't know how I forgive myself. I only know I do now, and

I am fulfilled. I forgive the failed me now. I am sorry. I love you. I forgive the poor thinking me in me. I am sorry. I love you. I forgive the mistakes in me. I am sorry. I love you. I forgive the anger in me. I am sorry. I love you.

I don't know how I accept me as forgiven. I only know that I do now, and I am fulfilled.

SECTION X
Live in Rich Abundance

Chapter Forty-Four

Increase Your Financial Flow

One day while practicing The One Command, I experienced an amazing event. In addition to the peace and calm that came as a part of my daily practice, I spontaneously had a vision of money, cash, and big denominations of bills and coins falling from the universe into my life.

They fell into my home, my back yard, my bank account, and into my pockets and pocketbook; there was a grand wind that brought this flow. I could hear the wind, see the flow coming to me, and feel the excitement in my nervous system and my body. It was a wonder and a great gift of a simple understanding that I would like to share with you now.

One of the easiest and simplest techniques for gaining your good in cash, connections, relationships, or health is to imagine that which you desire rushing toward you, coming toward you on the winds of the universe and dropping right into your environment, your home, your office, your life.

Imagine if you were to take the same equivalent energy that you apply when worrying and stressing about your finances, those ideas such as I don't have enough, or I may lose what I have, or someone could take what is mine from me.

If you were to concentrate the equivalent minutes and hours you spend imagining how badly everything could go, or how difficult it is, or how you are not one of the lucky ones, or any of the myriad possibilities in your worrisome ideas, if you were to take that same time, energy, and effort and imagine instead what you wish to create coming toward you, then you would increase in quantum measure your cash and your strong financial future.

This is not an affirmation. This is applying the energy that you already apply to worrying into another direction, a direction towards you for your good.

Imagine feeling, with the same amount of strength and resonance that you apply to a fearful thought of lack or loss, positive ideas of cash coming to you; imagine money and cash, and your good flowing right to you, flowing into your pockets, into your bank account, and into your life, and know that you deserve this financial good.

Imagine people enjoying paying you for what you do, and imagine receiving unexpected gifts of cash.

Imagine, more and more cash arriving for your benefit, and imagine yourself debt free. Actually imagine the flow of money coming toward you instead of going away to pay your bills.

Imagine Your Full Bank Account

We mostly imagine paying out what we owe and therefore see the flow of cash and prosperity running through our hands towards another destination. We constantly imagine paying the bills or worry about the bills we have to pay.

Yes, we have to tell the truth about our finances and know what is due. Make a list and write it down; then concentrate on seeing all that amount of cash and more rushing to you, into your environment, into your bank account, into your life.

When you imagine and visualize this cash and financial bonus and wealth coming to you, it does. Eventually, it does in such a profound way that you will find you always have more than you need to cover any and all bills and eventually pay off your credit cards and mortgages, with plenty of savings, and with large amounts of extra cash to spare.

When you are creating from your Source Mind, with the equal amount of emotion that you have expended in fearful thoughts, and in the equal strength of desire to attract cash to you, not only do you have that cash and financial good, you also have a greater sense of accomplishment and fulfillment within you.

Some of you already are masters in manifesting less than you desire and you can redirect that same energy into creating cash and surplus right now.

Start right now imagining that money, cash, and abundance are coming to you.

If you are rich and have enough money, then imagine what you want emotionally: peace of mind, security, and the knowledge that as a rich person you are safe and secure and appreciated in the world.

You can elevate the emotion of desire that you demonstrate for wanting an object, a material object, into a spiritual process, into a manifesting process by connecting to Source, Commanding your cash coming to you, and then imagining, with emotion, it coming right directly to you.

You can say, "If I use the same amount of emotion that I have when I want some material goods that I think I have to have, that must be in my life right now, and for which I cannot wait a moment longer, then I can transfer that same amount of emotion and feeling to that which I desire as good cash in my life, and that I must have right now, and be fulfilled."

As you continue to be in that resonance of desire of receiving and fulfilling yourself emotionally, and you combine that with going to

Source and Commanding that which you desire financially, you are able to have abundance, extra cash, and more than you need. You must. It is the Law of Attraction in Action!

If you think about it, it is insanity to energize your mind and body with fearful, hopeless thoughts of lack and debt, especially when you can change your financial circumstances in a moment, by redirecting every ounce of that same fear-power into prosperous thinking.

Money responds to your desire for it. Money wants to be with those who have a passionate desire and are sincerely interested in having it in their lives.

Know that you have the power to increase your cash, your financial good, and your peace of mind by focusing inward to your Source Mind, and from this state, you can create all the money, cash, and financial good that you could ever desire!

Go to Source and Command:

**I don't know how I turn my fear power into my manifesting power.
I only know I do now, and I am fulfilled!**

Chapter Forty-Five

Redirect Your Energy

The reason that we think money won't come, or that there isn't enough, or that it is for others but not for us, or that we'll lose what we have, is because we have been trained to think that way.

You have been trained to think that way, and it is up to you to retrain your emotional thinking about money.

Here is the simple truth: if you want to create the grand financial and emotionally prosperous life that is your birthright, and that you deserve, then redirect your energy to that result, and it will arrive.

Substance is everywhere! Prosperity is everywhere!
This one simple practice teaches you to apply the same

POWER and **ENERGY**

that you send into your universe when
you imagine financial loss and lack, and by

REVERSING THAT FLOW,

you see more income and greater financial sanity arriving daily in your life than you have ever imagined before.
It will arrive. It simply must!

You are the master of your life, creating your financial state now, and by reversing your thoughts and images, and applying the same amount of emotion into ATTRACTING money to you and KEEPING MONEY with you, it must manifest into a positive cash flow and great cash-rich savings and investments.

EVERY TIME THAT YOU HAVE A FEARFUL THOUGHT,

REVERSE THE FLOW.

Start with the simple statement:

I don't know how I reverse the flow.
I only know I do now, and I am fulfilled.

Use the Power of Your Emotions

Take all the fear that you project about not having money, or if you are rich, losing what you have, and focus that same energy to attract and regenerate what you need.

For example, what is the litany that you recite? I can't pay this; I don't have enough for that; when I do get some money, I worry that it will run out and that it will never come again.

When you reverse the flow of your fearful thoughts about money, instead of seeing money leave you to never return, you see that cash come to you and remain with you.

When you redirect the flow, you are applying the same fear energy that you are so used to in a different direction.

You are creating flow to you. You are already masters, and you can apply the same power of your own thinking that is maintaining your financial lack into creating your financial good.

You have the power of choice to reverse the flow!

Start right now to imagine what you desire in cash coming to you.

Imagine **three times** the amount that you want and more coming into your hands, into your bank account, and arriving in many unexpected ways.

**Focus your desire on that rich
substance arriving in your life, now!**

Yes, you do have those bills. Yes, you do have a mortgage or rent. Write them down, and make a record of your bills and debts and then ignore them in your thinking. Leave them alone. Yes, be realistic that you must and will pay those bills.

Reverse the flow, and imagine **three time**s the money that you want and more coming to you. Then you have plenty to pay those bills.

When you concentrate on the money leaving you and not having enough, then that is what you manifest.

It Is Simple and Easy

When you concentrate on money coming to you and remaining with you, then you have plenty, without stress.

It might feel uncomfortable at first because you are not used to attracting money to you, or imagining that you have plenty with grace, ease, and security. Yes, that might be uncomfortable in the cells of your body and in your thinking.

When you **reverse your fear, you reverse your emotions** from lack to abundance. Money must and does respond and honor your word and your declaration to the universe. It is the law. So, of course, money will appear on a daily basis in your life.

This is the simplest and **most powerful idea** you will ever discover about reversing debt, and increasing cash in your life.

THIS ONE PRACTICE
will literally reverse debt into prosperity,
and lack of cash into an abundant flow.

STOP AND IMAGINE MONEY FLOWING TO YOU!

Every day, unconsciously, when you are thinking about what you do not have in cash, and how far behind you are in your bills, and how much debt that you have, then your brain, your unconscious mind, and your Source Mind must keep repeating this experience for you.

START FOCUSING ON CASH COMING TO YOU.

Your subconscious mind is your biggest ally when you direct it to operate for you, consciously.

I don't know how I have three times my expenses in cash in my bank account at all times or more. I only know that I do now, and I am fulfilled!

Chapter Forty-Six

Money Comes to You

O ne spiritual teacher asked this question: How much longer in this lifetime do you want to have an experience of lack? Do you think maybe you have got the lesson of not having enough? Have you engaged in limitation and fear of losing what you have enough?

I think you've got it. What about the new learning, the experience of prosperity, of abundance, of manifesting cash and money in your life beyond what it is that you need? Are you ready for that? I think you are.

Here is a little exercise I think you'll enjoy.

Put your hands out in front of you and bring them back towards you as if you are scooping money up in your hands and bringing all that cash into you. Imagine it as a money shower that you pour over you. Have fun. Get loud. Command money's attention and it will arrive.

Money comes to me now. Money comes to me now. Money comes to me now. Money comes to me now. Money comes to me now. Money comes to me now. Money comes to me now. Money comes to me now. Money comes to me now. LOUDER! Money comes to me now. Money comes to me now. Money comes to me now. Money comes to me now. Money comes to me now. Money comes to me now. Money comes to me now. Money comes to me now. Money comes to me now. Money comes to me now. Money comes to me now. Money comes to me now. Money comes to me now. I am bathed and refreshed in money now.

I don't know how I have all the cash and more for me. I only know I do now, and I am fulfilled.

Money comes to me now. See the money coming in, pouring in on top of you. See it coming into your pocketbooks and pants pockets. See it coming into your bank account. See it in the cells of your body. See big denominations of bills. See coins, the cash, the checks, the dividends coming to you, coming to you, coming to you now, and I am fulfilled.

Now simply increase your energy, and see cash and money coming to you.

When cash comes to you, you have all the money required for bills. It comes to you; it is yours.

It comes to you; it is yours.

The habit of seeing it go out creates a F L O W away from you, and you want to create a F L O W coming to you as yours to have.

Wealth means that you have all the cash you need and more, and that the bills get paid simply and easily.

And you have more in your bank account than you ever imagined possible after the bills are paid.

And being cash-rich becomes so familiar that you don't have to worry about paying bills or mortgages because you have so much extra cash that you can spend what you want.

I don't know how money comes to me and stays with me and fills up my bank accounts. I only know that it does now, and I am fulfilled. I only know lots and lots of money is mine now, and I imagine and feel and smell and love all that cash. Learn to play with cash and to have fun with cash and have a great relationship with cash. When you say all that money is mine now, that is your power of who you are manifesting you good.

When reversing addictive poor thinking to prosperity thinking you are teaching your subconscious mind that there is a better way, another way, a prosperous way to live.

By applying The One Command, you can create a completely new financial, emotional, and stress-free life.

This knowledge is so simple, and it only takes moments—a few moments in your thinking to readjust your mind until this practice becomes as natural to you as your old way of thinking has been.

THIS IS A NEW TEACHING.
YOU ARE LEARNING ANOTHER WAY:
THE WAY OF COMMANDING YOUR WEALTH!

Your subconscious mind does not understand what you are asking it to do yet! Your subconscious mind is learning a new and better way to accomplish what you desire: to be cash rich and financially secure. That is, to be at ease over your finances, and to live in a balanced state of financial security, happiness, health, harmony, and joy

When you state The One Command, it is guaranteed that you can be as rich as you can imagine, as peaceful, and as financially and emotionally secure as you have always desired.

Again, instead of worrying about what you have to pay, and how big of a debt that you have,

IMAGINE MONEY FLOWING TO YOU!

The results are immediate. Cash will show up in unexpected ways, bills will be paid, and your debt will be decreased. It must.

Close your eyes right now and connect to Source and see, feel, and hear all the money that you desire coming to you.

IMAGINE MONEY FLOWING TO YOU!
IMAGINE CASH FLOWING TO YOU!
IMAGINE MONEY FLOWING TO YOU!
IMAGINE CASH FLOWING TO YOU!
IMAGINE MONEY FLOWING TO YOU!

Imagine that money comes into your bank account, into your wallet, and into your pockets, and shows up in unexpected ways.

Imagine that you have so much cash it flows like water and is contained in a lake of prosperity and is ever-present for you.

Imagine that good cash has conversations with you and whispers in your ear how much it loves to play with you and help you in your life.

Imagine all the good that you can have and be with the money you want right now.

Keep imagining it coming into your hands and it does!

Success Story

A very talented gentleman came to Commanding Wealth® at a time when he was in dire financial straits. He had been struggling in his video editing and promotional business, even though his products were of exquisite quality. His underlying emotional programs of sacrificing himself for others at his own expense kept him from attracting clients that paid him well and on time. As a consequence, he was deeply in debt and living on credit cards to make ends meet.

He began to Command for the emotional understanding of his value and worth. I don't know how I am worth being paid for what I do. I only know that I am now, and I am fulfilled. I don't know how my work is valued and I am well paid. I only know that it is so now, and I am fulfilled.

As he continued to Command for an emotional clearing and understanding of his worth, he released more and more old ideas and programs that arose to the surface.

In his own words, he shares his story:

I was hired as an audio technician to record Asara's Commanding Wealth® course in Dallas, Texas. I was over $42,000 in debt from unsecured credit cards and really didn't expect to gain much since I was working the audio levels of the recorder, which required my full attention. I felt like I was more of a casual observer, but I went through the moves and exercises as best as I could with the other classmates going back and forth from my post.

That's when my financial turnaround started. At first, I really didn't understand how money found its way to me in excessive amounts each and every month. It was so different than what I had experienced before. I began to receive an amazing deluge of jobs:

clients hired me to video, lay out, and design ads, billboards, and interiors, and they paid me on the spot. I only knew that money came to me from every direction I gave attention to, and it hasn't stopped since. The Commanding Wealth® formula taught me what I needed to know to live with income in excess of my expenses to the degree that I was able to pay big chunky payments to reduce my debt.

I continued to Command my financial good and the reduction of my debt and soon reported that I had paid off $12,000. I felt good about taking some pressure off my six-year old debt, but I really felt timid about the whole thing. I didn't know how to handle it. I felt like I was waking up for the first time. One would think that by paying off that amount of debt so quickly I would feel proud. Actually, I simply didn't feel good enough about myself yet—still seeing the $30,000 plus remaining debt and not knowing what was ahead.

I was birthing a new business with a machine that provides subtle energy to to help people. Not knowing how powerful the combination of the subtle energy from the machines and The One Command were, I continued with, I don't know how I sell two Tesla Light Photonic Machines a month. I only know I do now, and I am fulfilled. And what do you think happened? Yep, I sold more than two machines, helped a lot of people, and the money kept coming in.

My debt soon was reduced by another $10,000. Now I was down to $22,000 in debt. That was half of where I was at when starting to Command my wealth only months earlier. I felt more encouraged to move forward. I felt like I was on a roll and wanted to see the day I was able to report that ALL my debt was behind me.

I had been noticing my credit report worthiness scores were rising each month as I reduced my debt. I thought this was kind of funny, but this was beginning to be more real to me because I wanted to manifest buying a beautiful house. My debt reduction report stated that I had knocked off another $12,000. I was clearly moving out of debt and then Asara helped me clear even more limiting ideas and I began to Command selling ten systems a month. That's $160,000 in sales. I felt ready for that level of new wealth, and Commanded, I don't know how I sell ten systems a month. I only know I do now, and I am fulfilled. What do you suppose happened? I sold eleven units, and my debt was cleared! In addition, I was able to contribute $16,000 to charity, and as of today, when I am writing this ten months from the start of The Commanding Wealth® theta journey, I have commanded $90,000 in cash. All of my $45,000 debt is paid off with $20,000 cash surplus in the bank. Here is my new Command, I don't know how I create millions of dollars with my business, www. TeslaLight.com online. I only know I do now, and I am fulfilled. And trust me, as Asara says, If I can do it, you can too!

Chapter Forty-Seven

Live the Possibilities

A great attribute of the The One Command is the belief in what is possible. When you open you brain and your mind to what is possible, you return to a state of anticipation and excitement about what can happen.

There are unconsciously held beliefs that we can clear by the simple process of coming back to our desire, of coming back to our dream of what is possible by Commanding, I don't know how I have my house, I don't know how I have my clients, I don't know how I make this connection in the world with others. I only know I do now, and I am fulfilled.

When you are a master of your own destiny, you deny the limiting ideas of the outside world, and focus on what is possible instead, and when you do, you know a greater good and receive a greater capacity for success, wealth, and achievement than you originally imagined.

Action without Evidence

Every good action arrives from the notion that it may be possible. That greater good is so immense, so enormous, so much more than what we could even imagine that we have to turn it over to that greater part of ourselves with the desire to have it, even if we begin with it as only a possibility.

And then, when what we desire, and imagine as possible, arrives, it becomes our miracle.

You make this contribution to the world by involving yourself in the world, with these deeper practices within you, of knowing what it feels like to be a successful person with a great idea that the world receives gladly.

What would that feel like to be a good person with a great idea that the world receives gladly? To have that feeling that the world receives you gladly, that the world receives what you have to offer gladly, that they are waiting for you? What about that as a possibility?

The easy way to rich and secure living is to focus on what you want, and to know that it is possible. This is the mindset of wealthy, successful, and happy people.

I remember one Oprah story in which a twelve-year-old boy started a foundation with his lemonade stand, and he raised thousands of dollars for disaster relief. He was able to do this because he believed in the thought that he could.

Before you disenfranchise yourself from living a joyful, rich life, stop and think what you can do, rather than what you can't, and start at this very basic beginning in retraining your thinking, by going to theta and making The One Command, I don't know how I change my life to see what is possible. I only know I do now, and I am fulfilled.

What is beautiful about this practice is that you can return to that place of innocence where, in fact, like a child, you did not know the answer.

To practice your excellence and demonstrate your growth at any age, it is simple: you only need to ask by going to theta and stating The One Command, I don't know how I trust that there are endless possibilities in my life. I only know that I do now, and I am fulfilled.

Once you begin to ask for that understanding, it must come. You are attracting what you are thinking now, and this is no different. It is only different in that you are asking for something in a more elevated state of awareness, in a larger capacity, and in a greater desire. Once you remember that we are simple beings existing, breathing, and living in an enormous galaxy of endless potential, then you come to realize your own greatness in affecting your life.

Unlimited Supply

One young man, who was applying The One Command and imagining unlimited possible wealth, had an amazing miracle happen for him. I was talking to him and I asked, "How has your career been going since you took the One Commanding Wealth® program?" He replied, "I had set my goals for $650,000 for the year, and I made over $1.5 million, and I earned three-fourths of it in the last three months of the year, after the course."

He further explained that he had embraced the notion I taught—that billions and trillions and more dollars than we can imagine, exist in the world and are available to us; once he focused on that unlimited supply, he knew that he was thinking too small about what was possible for him to achieve.

He thought on what was possible in available money—how an unlimited richness exists in this world, and all he was required to do was to tune into that, to hold that as a truth in his reality.

He said, "I did. I held that as a truth in my reality, and I got clients that had bigger and bigger jobs, that had greater and greater salaries. I get paid on a percentage of salary for the executives we place, and that is how I made that extraordinary income."

He increased his flow, knowing that there is an amazing capacity of wealth, and he personalized it. Then it was his.

Live Your Greatness

Once you realize that your life is a miracle, right from the very start, with nothing added to you or subtracted from you, then anything and everything that you are doing in this moment is greatness.

Whatever is your capacity for imagining that "anything" is your greatness.

When you desire to expand what is possible for you, then know this one truth: you cannot know what you have not experienced.

Do not prejudge the possibilities of achievement, success, and your greater good, but rather stay open, with great expectancy, and allow something even more magnificent than your original thought to arrive.

When you begin where you are, and accept you with blemishes and all, then you are taking yourself on a journey of exploration.

If you desire to explore a life of greater wealth, health, and happiness, then you are taking yourself on that journey. There is no outside force that can change you; only you can change you, and you do not even get to know what it will be like at the destination. That is how grand an unlimited possibility exists.

Appendix

Six-Step Process Summation

Write the names of each of the Six Steps on a separate piece of paper.

1. Ground
2. Align
3. Go To Theta
4. Command
5. Expand
6. Receive with Gratitude

Place the six pieces of paper in a horizontal line on the floor. You are going to stand on each piece of paper, and as you do, follow the words being read to you. Stay on each step until you complete your experience, taking as much time as you need, then move sideways to the next step.

Before you step on Ground, think of something you wish to manifest in your life: more money, a car, better health, or a relationship. When you choose what you wish to manifest, first simply have the idea of what it is you would like to create for yourself. Now that you have that idea of what it is you would like to manifest, close your eyes and keep your eyes closed during the entire process. When your eyes are closed, you access different portions of your brain than when your eyes are open. You have a deeper experience when you keep your eyes closed.

Have your partner read these directions, slowly at each step, as he or she guides you through the Six-Step Process. Stay at each step as long as it takes until you know that you are ready to continue. You will know, energetically, when you have completed the experience before moving forward.

Step One: Ground

Listen to the sound of my voice, and feel the weight of your body settling down onto the paper under your feet. Now imagine roots coming out from the bottom of your feet and send them down, deep, deep into the Earth. Connect with the magnetic power of the Earth, the basis and foundation of all of our support, and imagine that you are wrapping your roots around the exquisite element of gold, diamonds, and rubies in the center of the Earth. Feel the power of that energy grounding you and balancing you. Stay here until you feel your body shift into a well-grounded state.

Step Two: Align

When you are ready, move sideways to the second step (your partner will hold your waist to guide you if necessary), and stand on Align.

Imagine all that power of the Earth's energy coming into your body, into your heart. Now take a deep breath, and as you exhale, imagine that the energy is expanding in all directions around you. The breath of your heart is expanding in all the directions, above and below and around in all directions. As you exhale, allow that breath to expand in all directions, aligning you with your purpose in a state of unconditional love. When you feel your body shift, you are ready to continue.

Step Three: Go to Theta

Now move sideways to the third step: Go to Theta. Imagine a golden beam of light, a field of energy flowing into you from the far distant reaches of the galaxies, flowing down through you and out below you, deep into the Earth. Imagine moving your consciousness up this beam of light, out the top of your head to above your head, out to the outer edges of the planet, on through the solar system, beyond the galaxy, until you push through the black void of space, into the white luminescence of Source. This is the place of creation of all that you desire. Think and feel from this state of consciousness as you activate your DNA, the cells of your body, and your mind to be that master that you are.

Step Four: Command

While holding the thought of what you wish to manifest, mentally and silently Command: I don't know how I _____ (fill in the blank) is manifested. I only know that it is now, and I am fulfilled! Take your time to allow this declaration to fulfill itself energetically in your body, before you move to the next step.

Step Five: Expand

While you are still in theta, imagine what you desire in a bigger way, a greater capacity, an expanded version that serves more good than your original idea. When you expand your idea to become something bigger than you, you increase its capacity to manifest. Allow yourself to let your idea take on its own energy. Observe as it changes and becomes even more than you can imagine. Watch as new, expanded, bigger ideas arrive. Let it become more beautiful and harmonious. Stay in the process until you know that it is done. Now that you are in this greater state of capacity, move to the sixth step.

Step Six: Receive with Gratitude

State in your mind clearly, "Thank you! It is so!" And experience the sense of gratitude and fulfillment emanating from you and coming into you from Source. While in this state of gratitude, move your consciousness back down the golden beam of light, coming gently and respectfully back into your physical body, and imagine the particles of consciousness of your manifestation floating down from Source into your body, into the cells of your body, and into your DNA itself. Imagine unwinding, unwinding, unwinding all the old limiting ideas and rewinding, rewinding, rewinding, a new holographic image of your great good. Imagine a new holographic image of this life that is your new life replicating itself in every DNA strand in your body, in every organ of your body, in every hair follicle of your body, and in every particle of emotion in your body and your thinking. Feel it, accept it, and give thanks again. Thank you! It is done! It is so!

Take a deep breath, and send your energy back down into the

Earth to firmly reestablish your ground of being. Adjust your energy; let your body stretch, flex, and move with this new understanding of reality. Take all the time you need to come once again fully awake and alert into your body. Open your eyes, and return to the room.

Note: If you are doing this process by yourself, you may wish to sit and record some of your ideas, thoughts, and feelings afterwards. If you are doing this process with a friend, then share what it is that you discovered.

To train yourself in this process, I recommend that you repeat this at least twice the first time you do it. Practice going through the process every day until it becomes so natural for you that you can go through the Six Steps mentally, instantly, any time that you wish to concentrate on what you want to manifest. Practice until this becomes an unconscious internal process.

Join us at www.CommandingWealth.com
for information on our

One-Day The One Command Events
Commanding Wealth® Seminars
Free Learning Web Section
Weekly Free Teleconferencing
Elearning for Success Program

Commanding Wealth®
Rural Delivery
PO Box 1409
Langley, WA 98260 USA